Automated
Day Trading Strategies

Highly Profitable Algorithmic Trading Strategies for the Crypto and Forex Markets

Contents

Introduction

Do you want to make money trading the markets, but don't have the time to sit in front of your computer all day long? In this book we will take a look at some of the best automated day trading strategies and explore how to use them to make a profit.

What is Day Trading? Before we get into the different automated trading systems available today, it's important that we understand what a day trader actually is. A day trader is simply someone who buys and sells cryptocurrency or other financial instruments during the course of a day. They are not interested in holding these securities for an extended period of time, but instead aim to make small profits on a number of trades throughout the day.

This type of trading requires a lot of attention and vigilance, as traders must be constantly watching the markets and making quick decisions about whether to buy or sell. It can be a very profitable way to trade, but it's also one of the most challenging ways to make money in the market.

What is Automated Trading?

With automated trading, you take all the emotion out of trading. Instead of sitting at your computer all day long watching charts and trying to make tough decisions, you simply set up your trading system to do it for you. All you have to do is sit back and watch as the profits roll in!

In this book you'll learn how you can use algorithmic trading strategies to trade crypto and create your own trading bot (without coding) to remove emotions from the equation so that you make consistent profits regardless of what's going on in the market.

I've also included all of my most effective crypto day trading strategies as well as an easy-to-follow blueprint which shows exactly to execute the trading strategies. Whether beginner or expert trader, these are simple yet powerful strategies that can greatly increase your PNL.

There are many advantages to automating your trades, including:

Increased consistency - Automated trading removes the human emotion from the equation, so you can make trades in a consistent manner regardless of market conditions.

Increased profitability - By using automated trading systems, you can take advantage of opportunities that you may not have had time to trade manually.

Reduced risk - Automated trading helps reduce risk by implementing predetermined stop losses and limits.

Faster execution - Automated trading systems can execute orders much faster than a human trader, allowing you to take advantage of opportunities as they arise.

So now that we know what automated trading is and some of the advantages it has over manual trading, let's get started!

Chapter 1: The Basics of Automated Trading

Automated Trading Strategies (ATS) are algorithms that typically use technical indicators to identify high probability price movements. Once a signal is identified, an order is placed and executed on the market. The user does not need to monitor their account constantly as the ATS ensures that all trades are carried out within predefined parameters such as stop losses or profit targets. ATS removes emotional decision making from trading analysis and execution.

Algorithms are able to produce remarkable returns during turbulent times by acting on raw data with little human interference or emotion. A trading algorithm is a set of trading instructions that can be written in any computer language.

How Automated Trading Works

A typical automated trading strategy will rely on specific technical indicators, that have been modified to give the most accurate entry and exit signals possible. When creating a new ATS it is important to optimize the parameters of the indicators in your strategy through backtesting and simulated trading.

There are three main types of automated trading strategies: arbitrage, trend following and mean reversion. The strategies in this guide will be focused on trend following and mean reversion strategies; however, it is important to understand that some strategies may incorporate more than one trading strategy.

There are three different ways price can move on the markets: up (bullish), down (bearish) or sideways (sideways). An upward trend often occurs when there is positive momentum in the market, and prices will most likely continue to rise. Similarly, a downward trend occurs when there is negative momentum in the market and it is likely that prices will continue to fall. Trend following strategies attempt to capitalize on these trends by making trades based on momentum and price movements.

Mean reversion strategies are best used when the market is moving sideways, this type of market is characterized by little movement in prices, or choppy price action. Mean reversion trading is the process of buying an instrument when it is trading below its mean, or average price, and selling when the instrument trades above the mean. The idea behind this strategy is that short-term prices are unlikely to deviate too far from their long term average; therefore, you can profit by buying low and selling high.

There are many advantages associated with automated trading strategies:

- You don't need to monitor your market positions constantly meaning you can allocate more time to other activities - an ATS will constantly monitor the markets for new opportunities without any manual intervention required.

- They provide greater discipline as they will only make trades within pre-defined parameters.

- You can easily backtest your strategies and optimize your parameters to increase profitability.

Creating a Automated Trading Strategy

All automated trading strategies are based on a set of strict rules for entering and exiting each trade. These rules can be as simple as high-low trend filtering, or as complex as the cross-referencing of 3-5 indicators and several moving averages.

To create a simple trading strategy, we can base our trade on two inputs:

Entry Rules - The conditions that must be met in order the trade to be executed. This can be as complex or restrictive as you like (for example, 50% of several indicators must agree on a certain signal before entering a trade).

Exit Rules - The conditions that must be met in order for this rule to be true. This can also be as complex or restrictive as you like (for example, a 5 exponential moving average must cross the support line before selling).

These two inputs are combined to form our simple trading strategy - If entry conditions are met, then enter trades and exit once all exit conditions are met or a stop loss is triggered.

A simple example of how this would look would be:

- Enter trade when the RSI(14) is oversold AND the 5 period SMA crosses up through the 10 period SMA.

- Exit trade if the RSI is oversold OR the 5 SMA crosses below the 10 SMA

A correctly implemented Entry Rule ensures that you always buy at the lowest price. Exit Rules are more difficult to get right, since they determine when you actually exit a trade in profit. The Exit Rule is harder because it requires you to take other factors into account besides the price, such as volatility and risk/reward ratio.

High-low trend filtering

High-low trend filtering is one of the simplest trading algorithms; an example of this would be buying when the price is above the moving average, and selling when it falls below. These strategies are mostly used for market entry signals, but can also be used to exit a trade if you set your STOP LOSS below the last swing low of the asset during an uptrend or above the high during a downtrend .

Advanced trading algorithms

There are many other trading strategies that can be implemented in automated trading, such as breakout systems and relative strength index. The possibilities are endless when you combine technical indicators with a bit of creativity! Think about all of the information that is available to us - price, volume, time frame, moving averages, RSI - and then decide on a strategy that suits your needs.

Once you have decided on a set of rules , test out the algorithm using historical data. Backtesting is simply testing your trading strategy by applying it to past market data to see how well it would have performed if applied in the real world. After all, past performance does not necessarily indicate future results!

Chapter 2: Algorithmic Entry/Exit Signals For Automated Trading Strategies

In this chapter, we will cover the various types of signals that can be used to initiate and exit trades automatically. There are many different signals that can be used, but we will focus on the most profitable ones.

First, let's look at how to enter a trade using an automated system.

Types of Automated Trading Systems

There are many different automated trading systems but they can fall into one of three categories:

Trend-Following Systems

A trend-following system is a system that tries to catch the beginning of a trend and hold onto it until it shows signs of reversal. The classic example is moving averages crossover system, in which you buy when short-term moving average crosses above long term moving average and sell when it crosses below.

There are many different types of trend-following systems, but all of them rely on indicators to determine when a security has begun trending.

Breakout Systems

A breakout system enters trades after price has broken through some level of resistance or support, such as previous high/low or Bollinger band levels for example. A good breakout trading strategy would work best in volatile markets because these types of markets tend to have larger movements that last longer periods than range bound markets (where prices move sideways).

Mean Reversion Systems

The basic idea of a mean reversion strategy is that prices tend to move back towards the mean or average over time, so by buying when prices are below the mean and selling when prices are above the mean, you can profit from these signals.

There are many different indicators that can be used for this purpose, but one of the most popular is the Relative Strength Index (RSI).

So those are three common types of signals that can be used in automated trading strategies. In the next chapter, we will look at how to combine these signals together into an effective strategy.

The Most Profitable Automated Entry/Exit Signals

The following list of oscillators are some of the the best oscillators I have found on TradingView. These are indicators that the TradingView community has created.

To find these indicators on TradingView:

- Go into the "Indicators & Strategies" window on
- Click on the "Community Scripts" tab.
- Type the name of the indicator in the search box

"

These oscillators provide very accurate buy and sell signals, and are great for combining into a trading strategy.

Entry/Exit Signal #1: Scalp Pro

Author: ovelix

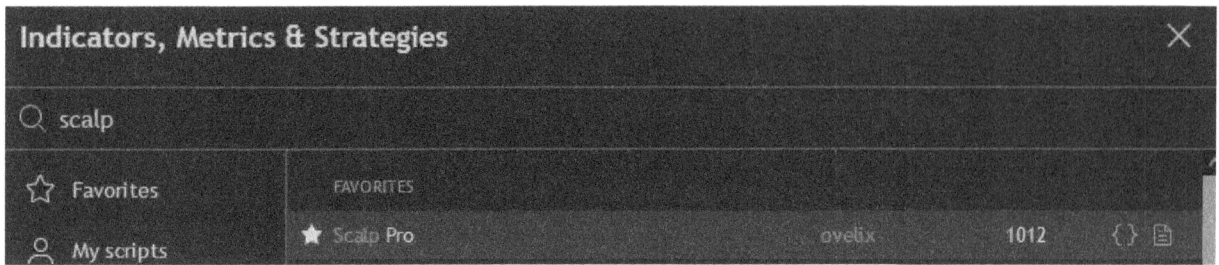

Search "Scalp Pro" in the indicator search box on TradingView to find this indicator

How it Works:

This indicator is based on modified MACD calculations and is displayed as a crossover oscillator with two lines, one fast and one slow (similar to a stochastic). Signals are generated when the fast line crosses above or below the slow line.

This indicator is great for scalping, it produces frequent signals most of which are accurate. The buy and sell signals will appear as labels on this indicator making it easy to use. This indicator works well in volatile market conditions.

Tip: In the indicator settings change the smooth length to 10 to reduce the amount of false signals

Buy Signal:

- The fast line crosses above the slow line and a green buy label appears

Sell Signal:

- The fast line crosses below the slow line and a red sell label appears

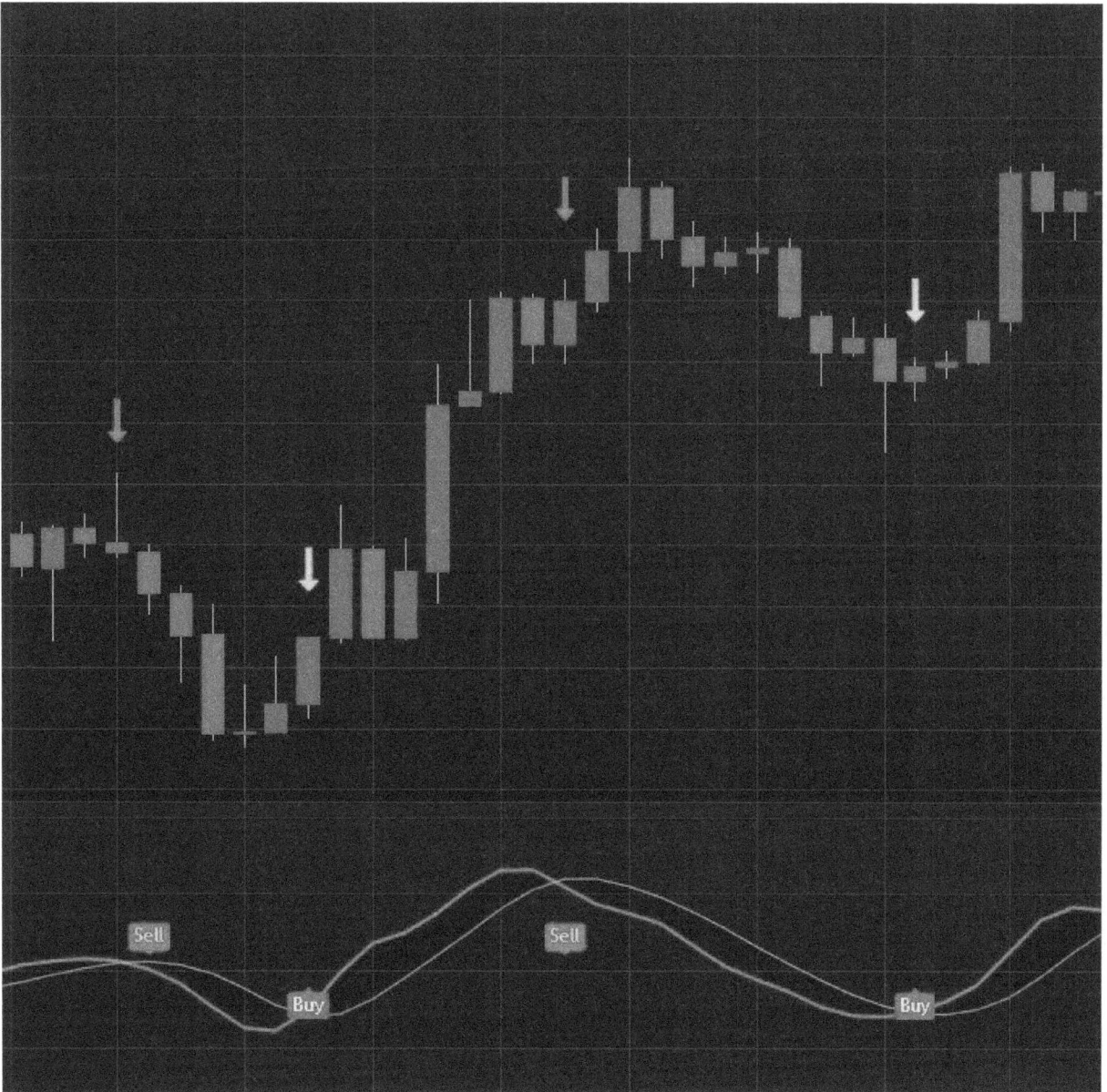

Example of buy (green arrow) and sell (red arrow) signals using this indicator

Entry/Exit Signal #2: Stochastic Weights - Basic

Author: BigBitsIO

To find this indicator type in "Stochastic Weights - Basic", in the indicator search box on TradingView

How it works:

This indicator is similar to a normal stochastics with a %K and %D line. When the stochastic moves above 80 it is considered overbought and below 20 is oversold. This indicator can give more accurate signals then a regular stochastic since it includes other values in its calculations.

Tip: I recommend enabling all of the stochastics in the indicator settings

Buy Signal:

- The %K line crosses above the %D line while under 50

Or

- The stochastic above 20 after being oversold

Sell Signal:

- The %K line crosses below the %D line while above 50

Or

- The stochastic crosses below 80 after being oversold

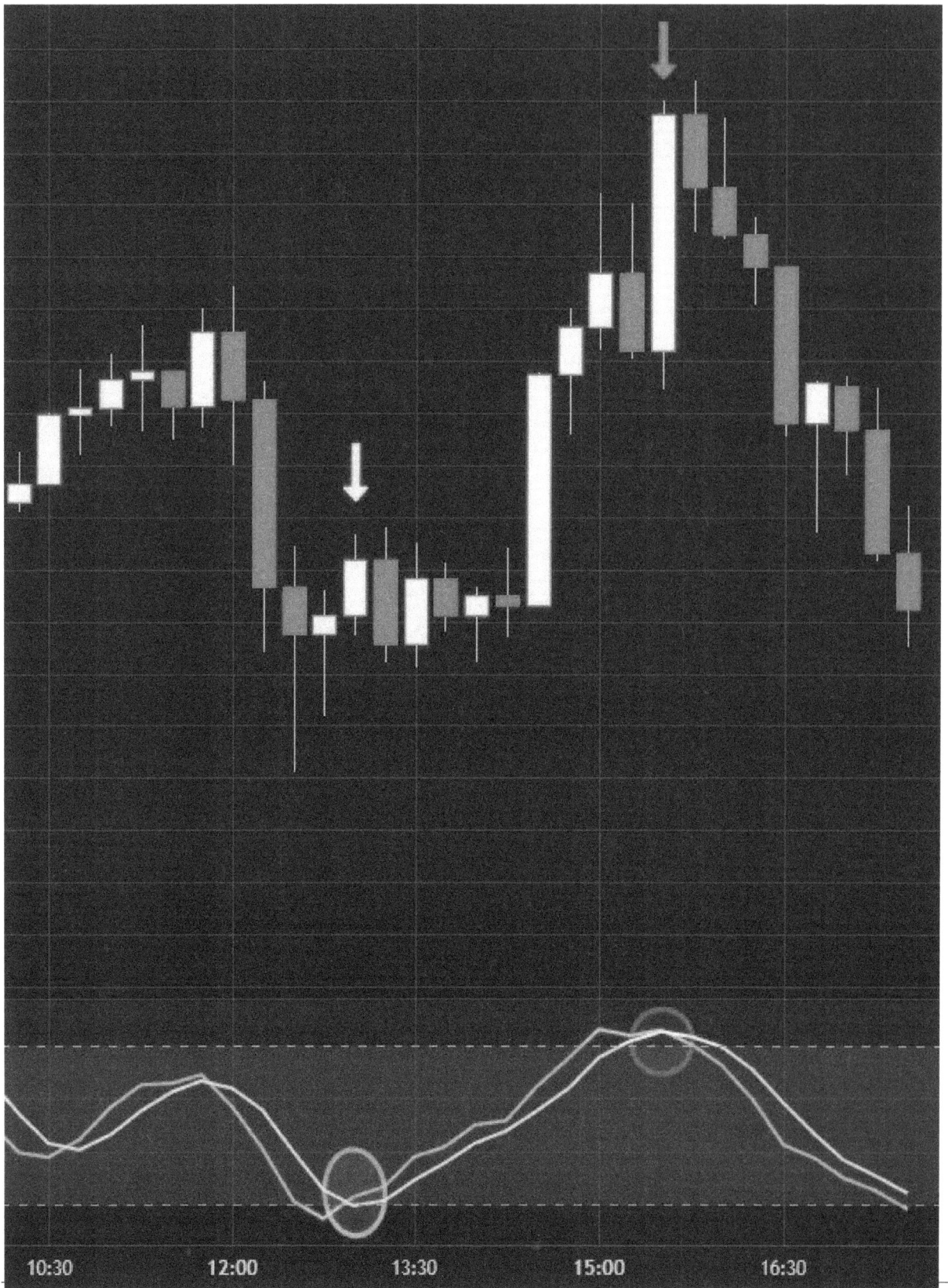

An example of buy (green arrow) and sell (red arrow) signals using this indicator

Entry/Exit Signal #3: Boom Hunter Pro

Author: veryfid

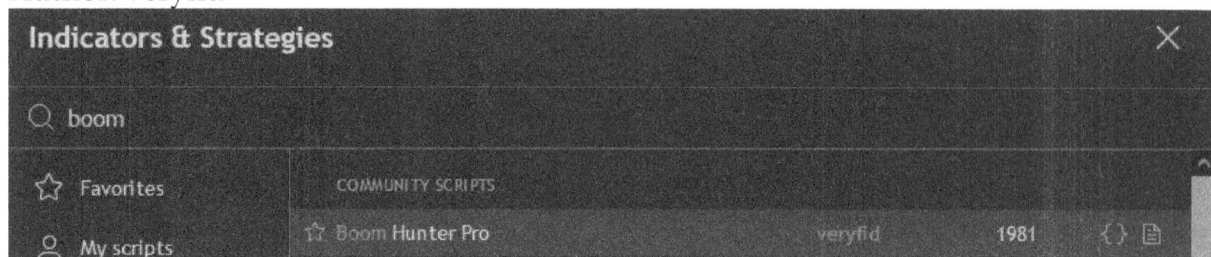

Search "Boom Hunter Pro" in the indicator search box on TradingView to find this indicator

How it Works:

This is an oscillator displays two lines that cross over similar to a stochastic indicator but it uses a number of different calculations to produce overbought and oversold signals. This will display buy and sell signals as green and red dots.

Buy Signal:

- Green dots appear on the oscillator

Sell Signal:

- Red dots appear on the oscillator

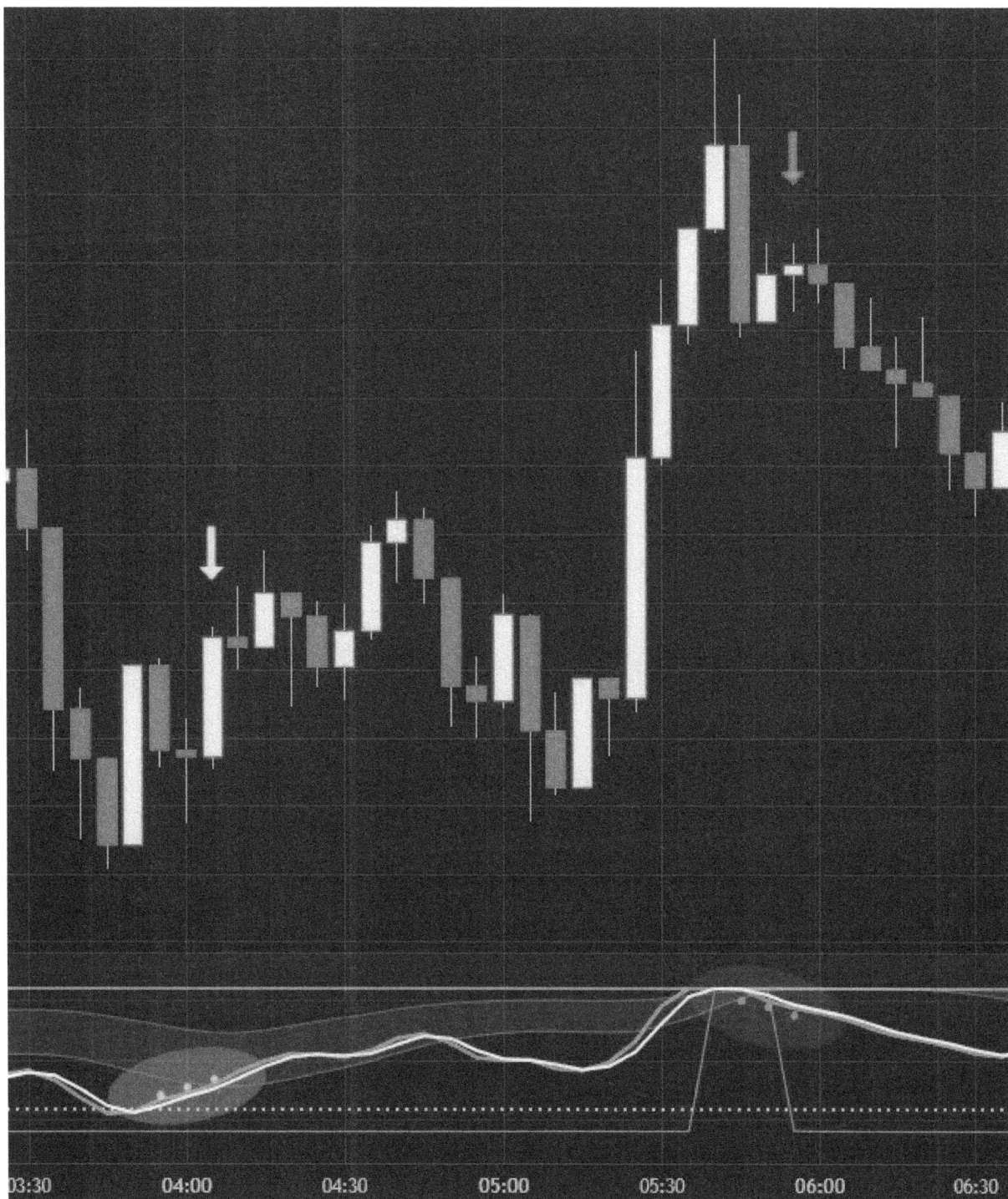

Example of buy signals (green circle) and sell signals (red circle) using the Boom Hunter Pro indicator

Entry/Exit Signal #4 Quantitative Qualitative Estimation QQE

Author: KivancOzbilgic

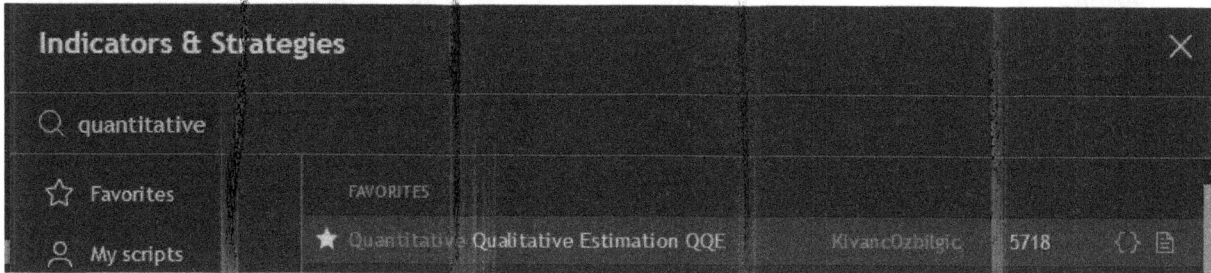

Search "Quantitative Qualitative Estimation" in the indicator search box on TradingView to find this indicator

What is it?

This indicator combines the RSI with the two ATR lines, when the ATR lines cross this provides buy and sell signals. This indicator will display buy and sell signals on it making it easy to use.

You can also use overbought and oversold levels on this indicator for signals with below 30 being oversold and above 70 being overbought.

Buy/Long Signal:

- When the fast line crosses above the slower line

Sell/Short Signal

- When the fast line crosses below the slow line

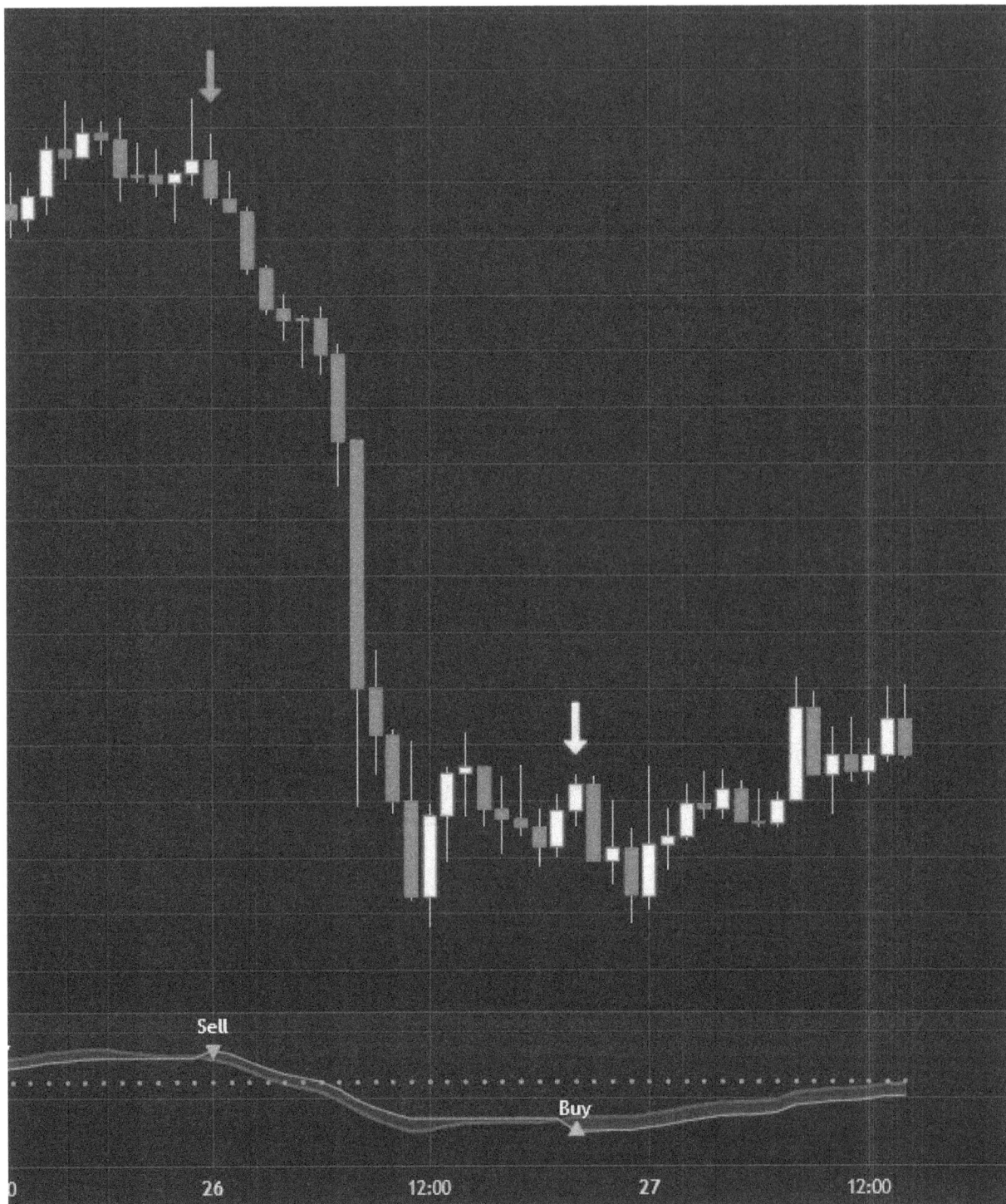

Example of buy and sell signals using this indicator

Entry/Exit Signal #5: [SK] Custom Klinger Oscillator

Author: sirkriz

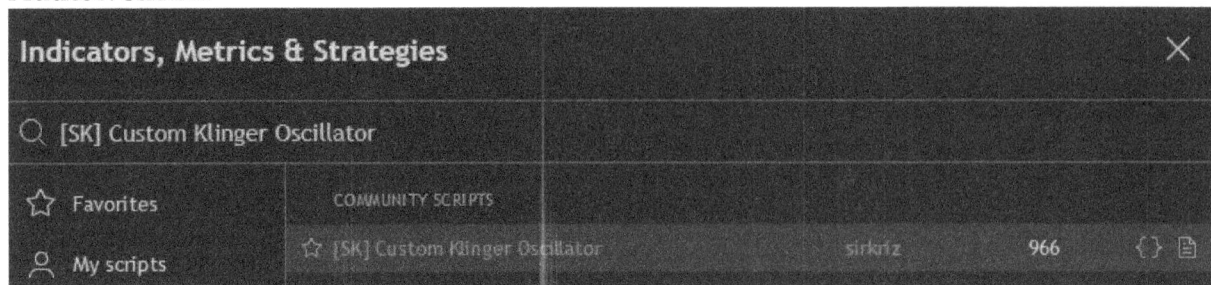

Search "[SK] Custom Klinger Oscillator" in the indicator search box on TradingView to find this indicator

How it Works:

This is a modified version of the Klinger oscillator. The Klinger oscillator is a volume based indicator and consists of two lines - one fast MA (moving average) and one slow. Signals will be generated when the two lines crossover. The zero line on this indicator can also be used to confirm downtrends and uptrends.

Tip: I recommend changing the **signal length to 12** to reduce false signals (uncheck the "use default values" box first).

Buy/Long Signal:

- The fast MA crosses above the slower one
- The fast MA turns green

Sell/Short Signal:

- The fast MA crosses below the slower

- The fast MA turns red

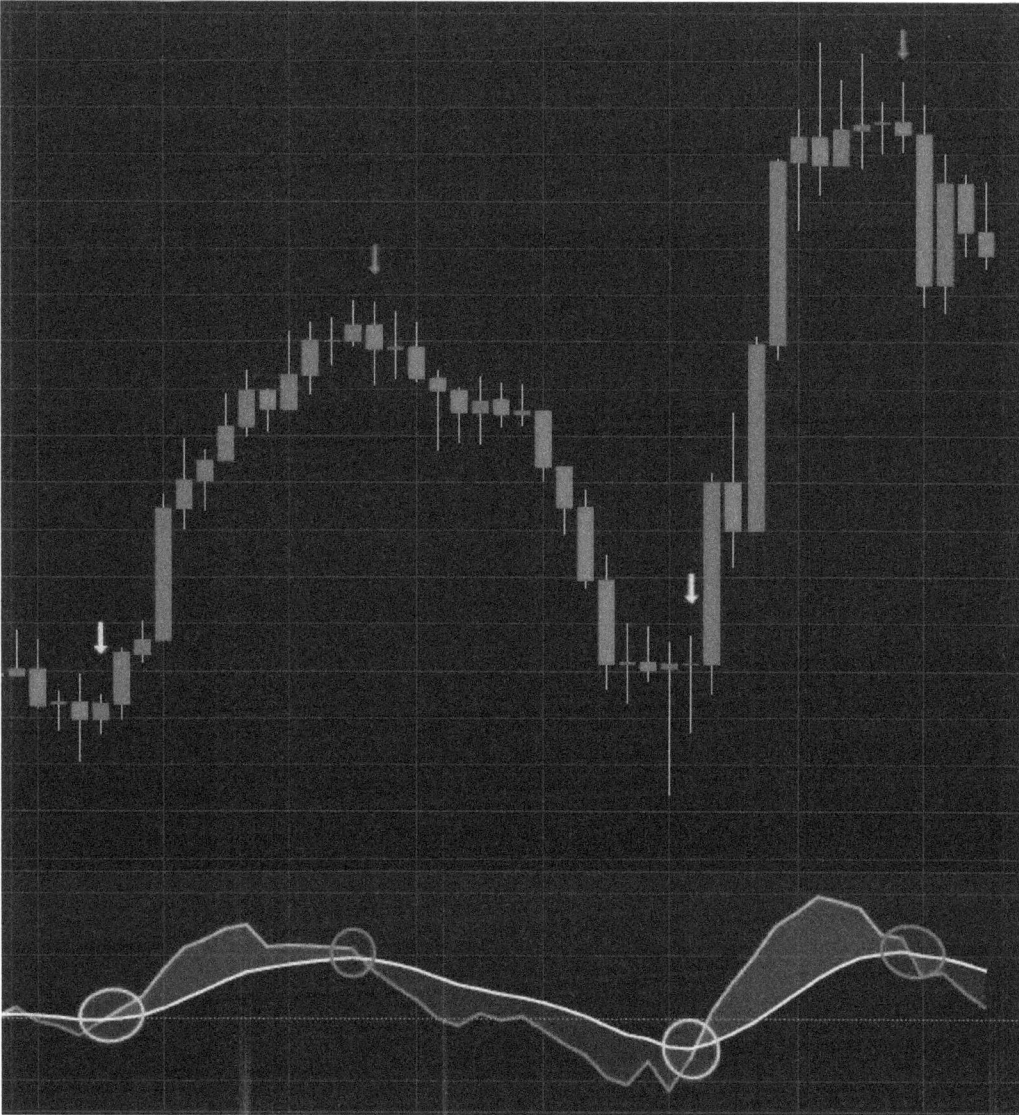

Example of buy signals (green circles) and sell signals (red circles) using the [SK] Custom Klinger Oscillator

Entry/Exit Signal #6: Stochastic Histogram

Author: nboone

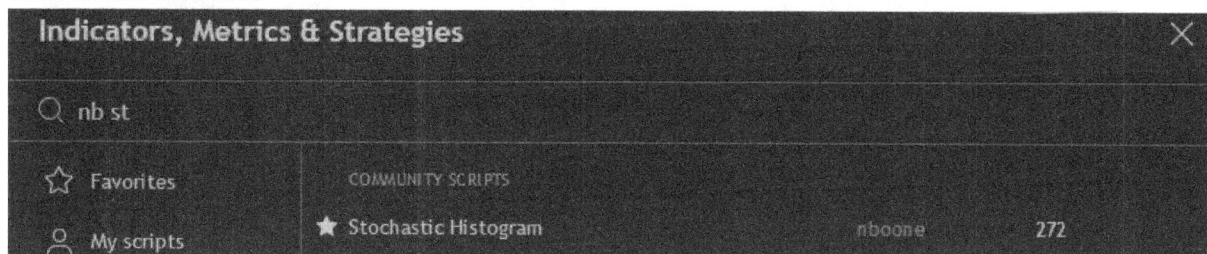

Search "Stochastic Histogram" in the indicator search box on TradingView to find this indicator

How it Works:

This indicator is a regular stochastic that is displayed as a histogram. Buy and sell signals will occur when the stochastic crosses the zero line.

Buy/Long Signal:

- The stochastic crosses above the zero line
- The histogram turns green

Sell/Short Signal:

- The stochastic crosses below the zero line
- The histogram turns red

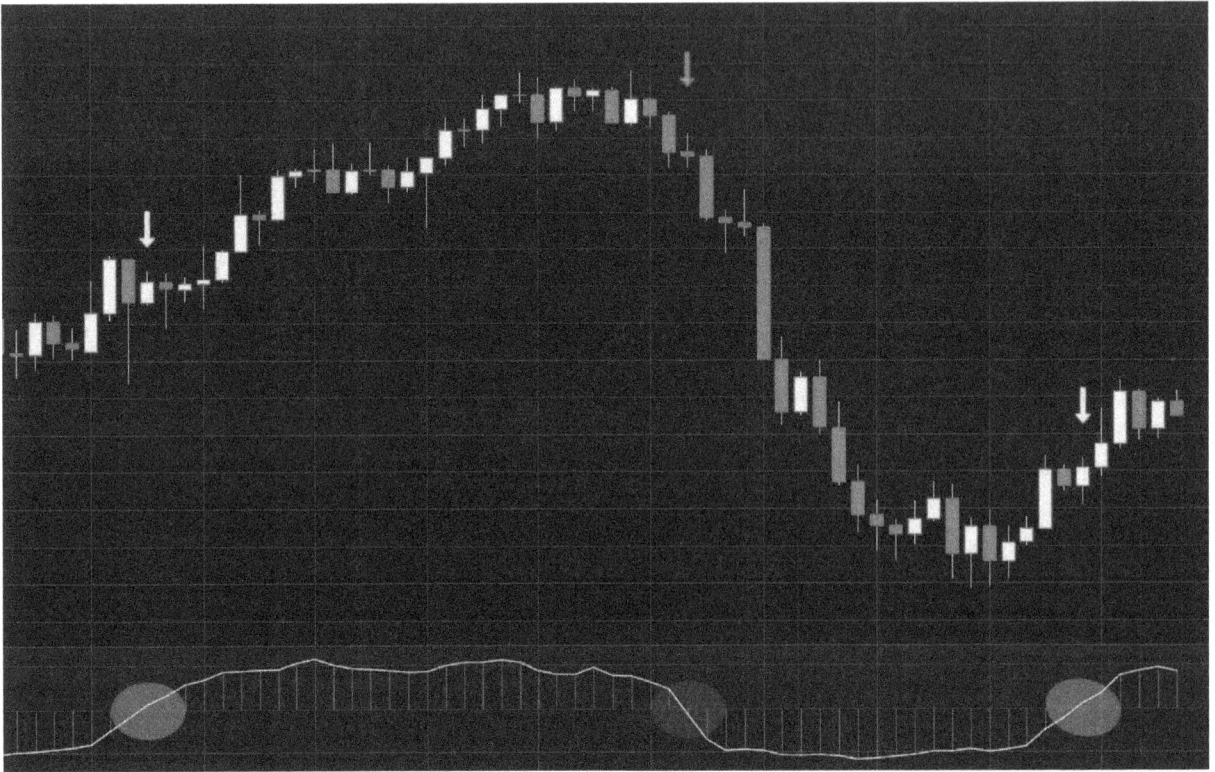

Example of buy signals (green arrows) and sell signals (red arrows) using this indicator

Entry/Exit Signal #7: Normalized Smoothed MACD

Author: Dreadblitz

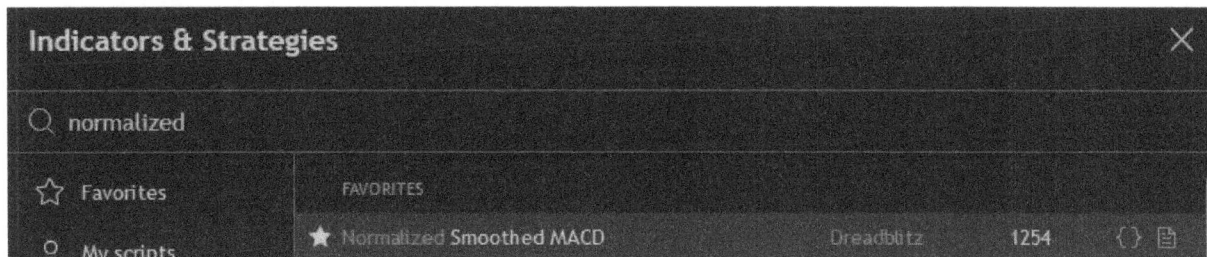

Search "Normalized Smoothed MACD" in the indicator search box on TradingView to find this indicator

What is it?

This indicator is an improved version of the MACD indicator, and provides more reliable entry and exit signals then a regular MACD. Two lines are displayed on this indicator, the signal line and MACD line

Buy/Long Signal:

- The MACD line is below the zero line
- The MACD crosses above the signal line and the MACD line turns green

Sell/Short Signal:

- The MACD line is above the zero line and turns red

Chapter 3: Creating a Automated Trading Strategy without Coding (simple method)

Most trading bots are created using coding, however there is one way you can make your own bot using signals from TradingView, without coding.

To use this method you will need:

- TradingView account

- Trading account on Binance or FTX exchange

- Create an account on https://capitalise.ai/

How to use Capitalise.ai

Capitalise.ai is a free platform you can use to make a cryptocurrency trading bot. It will execute your trades and also allows you to simulate your strategy as well as backtesting it (currently only on FTX version).
Using capitalize.ai is very simple; you just type your trading strategy in the strategy box. You first type in your buy conditions, then exit conditions.

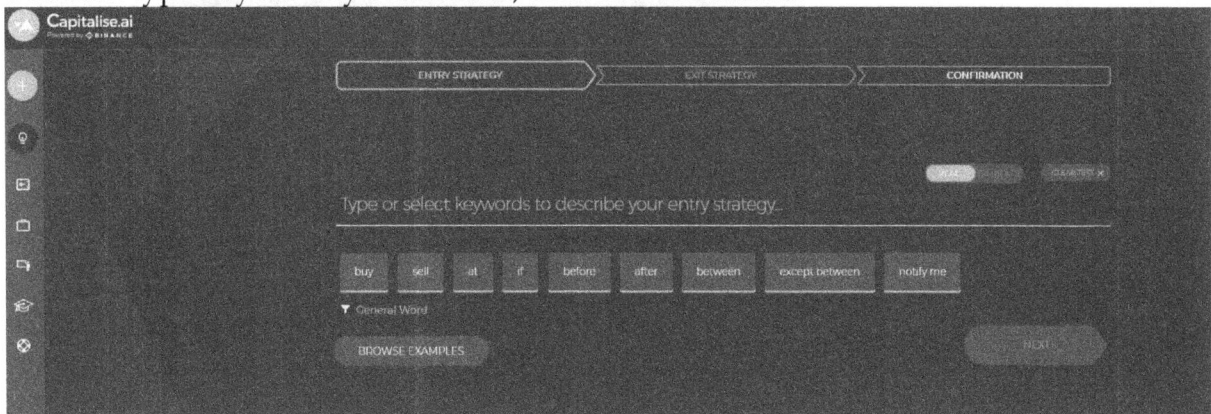

You can use the built in indicators on capitalise.ai to make a strategy, or you can use indicators or strategies from TradingView. To do this you copy **webhooks** on TradingView into capitalize.ai to generate buy and sell signals.
TradingView webhooks are simply TradingView alerts that get sent to capitalise.ai for entry and exit signals.

How to use TradingView Webhooks on Capitalise.ai

Step 1: Choose Your Entry and Exit Signals

First select a strategy or indicator you want to use on TradingView for buy and sell signals. This can be any indicator such as moving average crossovers or RSI signals. Add the indicator/strategy on your TradingView chart. I will use a MACD on TradingView as an example.

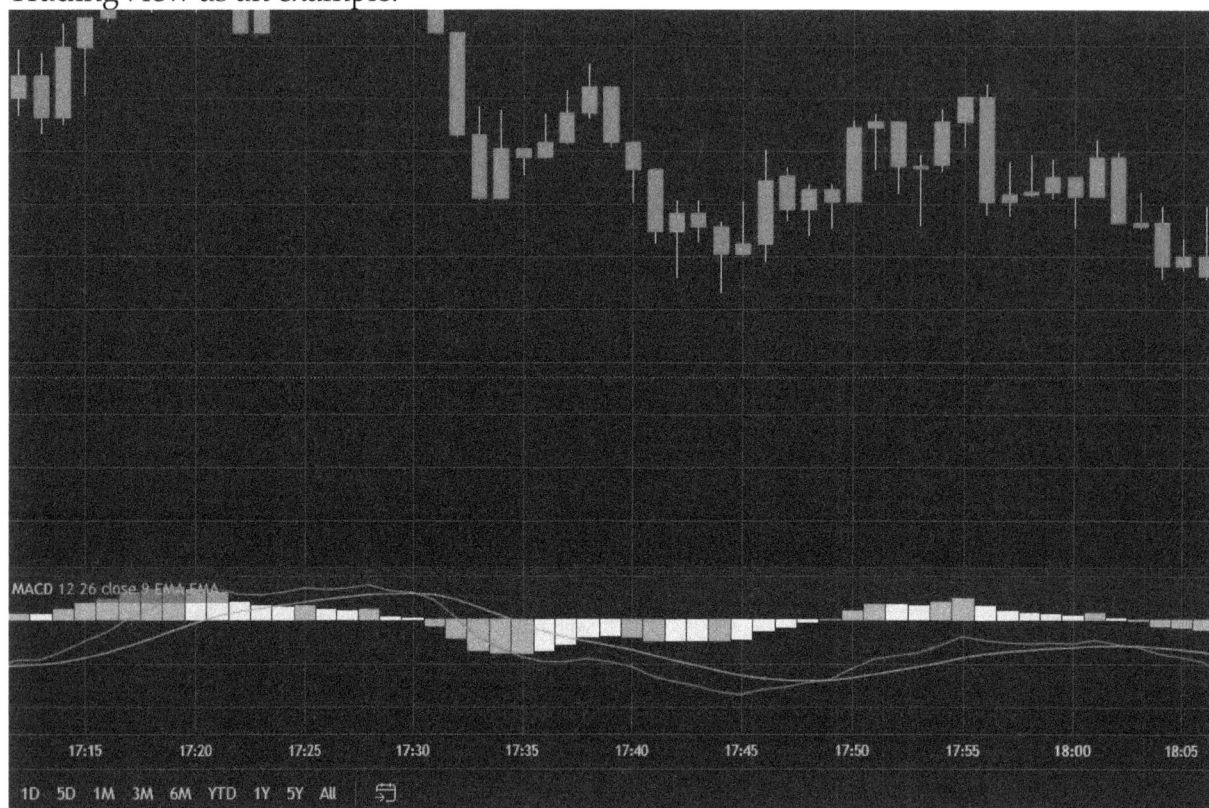

Step 2: Create a webhook link on Capitalise.ai

Once you have selected a indicator or strategy, create a new strategy on capitalise.ai, in the strategy box type in "if webhook triggers".

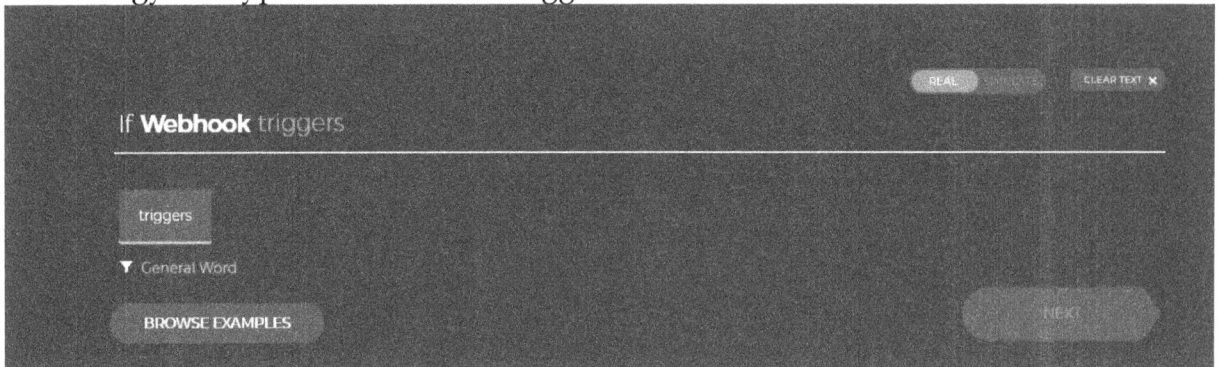

After typing in the full command, click on the word "webhook", you should see a small box pop up with two lines.

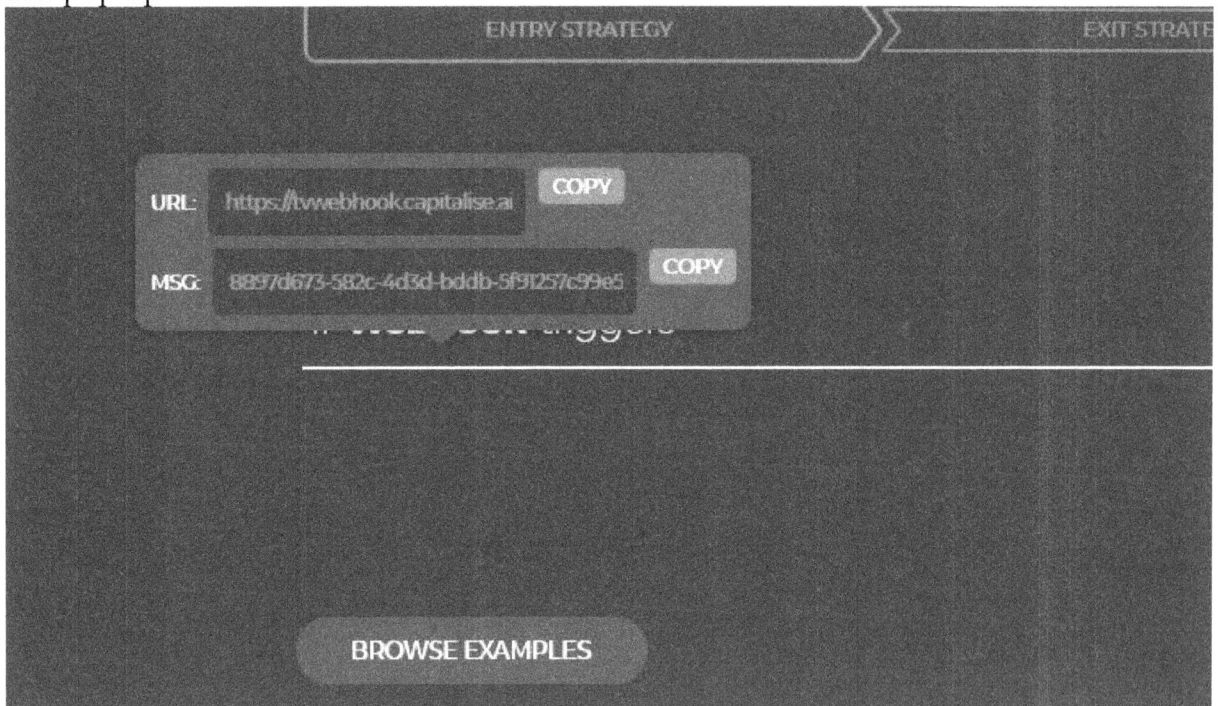

The first line "URL" and the second "MSG".

Step 3: Create an Alert on TradingView

Now go back to your TradingView chart, and add an alert on the indicator you want to use.

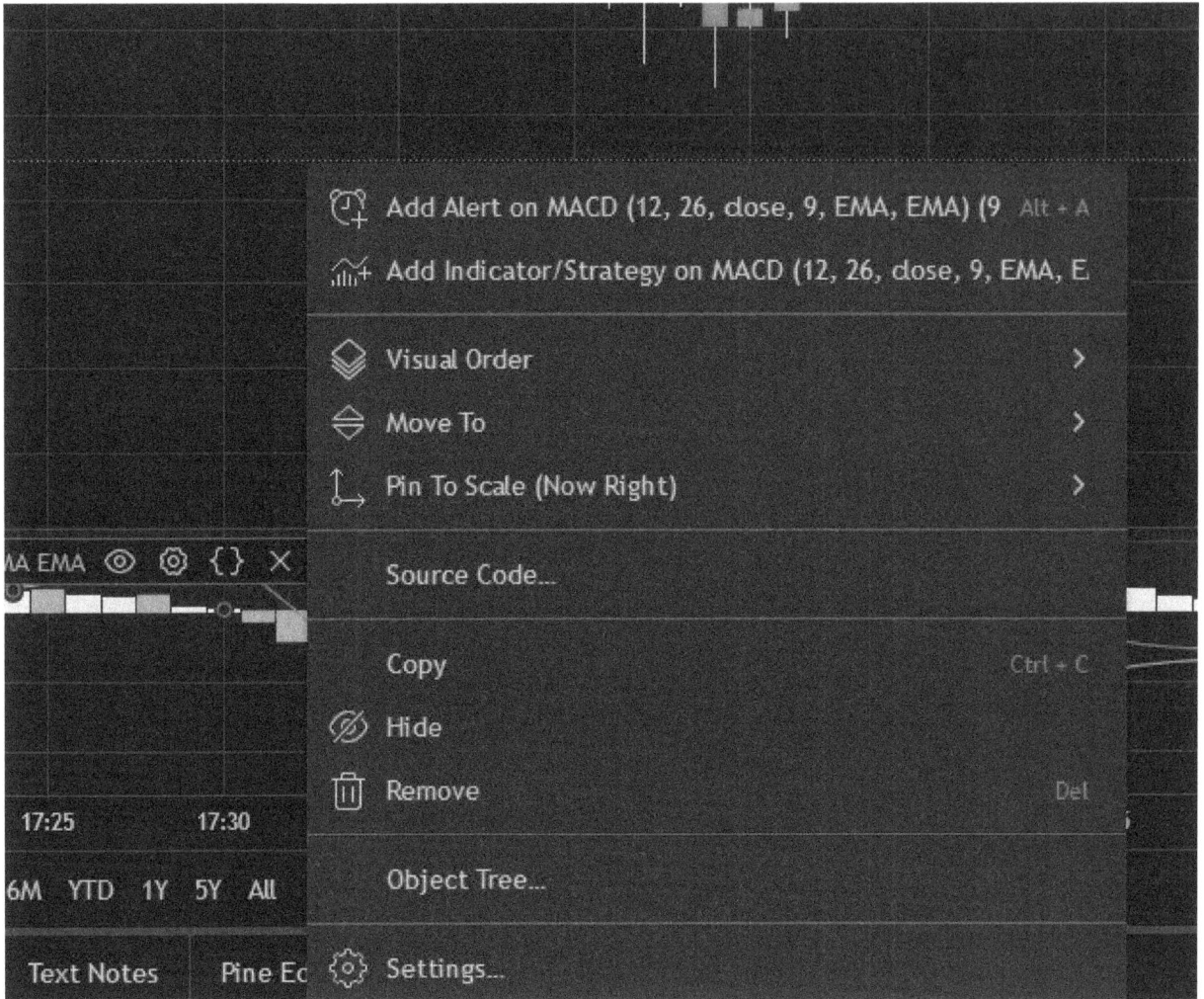

The alert box will pop up, in the alert you can adjust your alert settings. I have changed my alert to trigger when MACD line crosses above the signal line, this will be my buy signal. I also changed it to trigger **once per bar close**. I have also named my alert "MACD – Buy", just so I know what the alert is for later.

Make sure the webhook URL box is checkmarked.

Create Alert on BTCUSDT, 1m ×

Condition	MACD (12, 26,... ▾	MACD ▾
	Crossing Up ▾	
	MACD (12, 26,... ▾	Signal ▾

Options

| Only Once | Once Per Bar |
| Once Per Bar Close | Once Per Minute |

Expiration time 2021-12-27 📅   12:28 🕐

☐ Open-ended

Alert actions

☐ Notify on app

☐ Show pop-up

☐ Send email

☑ Webhook URL ⑦

https://tvwebhook.capitalise.ai

∨ More actions

Alert name MACD - buy

Message {"alertId": "00981c4d-3be5-4a66-baaa-2bad7d901acd"}

Cancel   Create

Step 4: Copy the Webhook Links into your Alert

Copy the URL link from capitalise.ai and paste it into the Webhook URL box on the TradingView alert and also copy the MSG from capitalise.ai and paste it in the alert message box on TradingView.

Step 5: Complete the Entry/Exit Conditions on Capitalise.ai

Then click create. Once the alert is active we can go back to capitalise.ai and finish typing in our buy conditions.

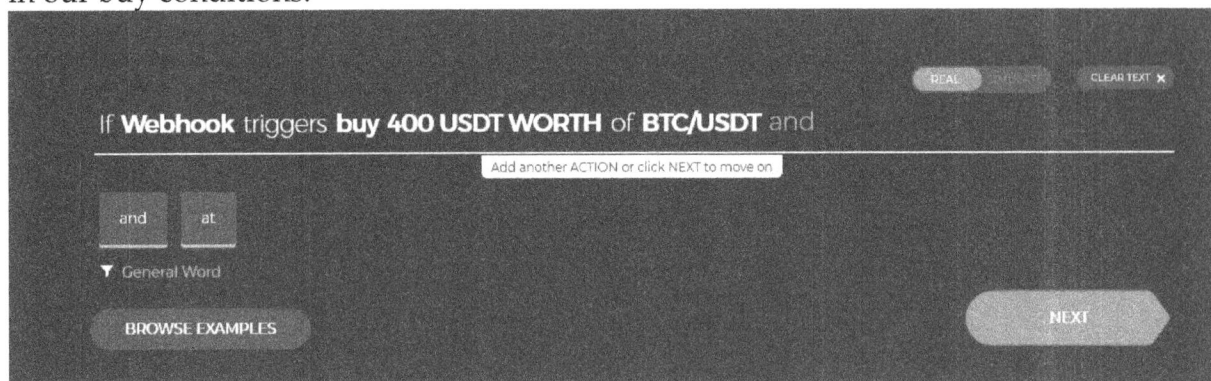

For my buy conditions I have typed in "If webhook triggers buy 400 usdt of btc". This means my trading bot will buy $400 of bitcoin if the MACD crosses up. You can add more conditions on top of your webhook if you want, but for this example I will keep it simple.

Exit Conditions

The same process can be used for your exit conditions.

- Create your exit alert on TradingView

- Type in "If webhook triggers", in the Capitalise.ai exit conditions box.

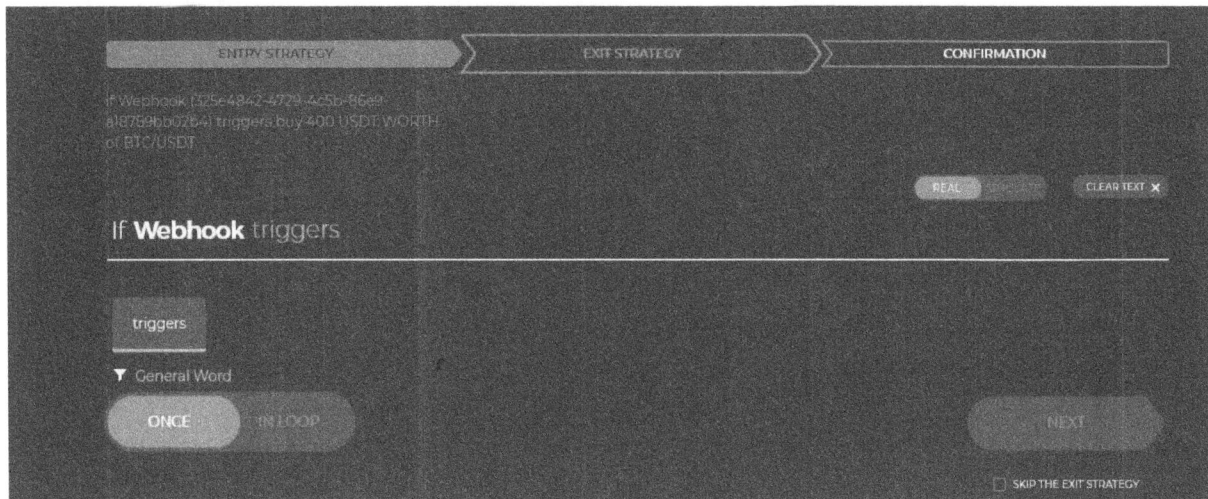

- Make sure to copy the new MSG link and URL into your TradingView alert box

Important – The MSG link for your exit conditions will be different than the one you used for the buy conditions

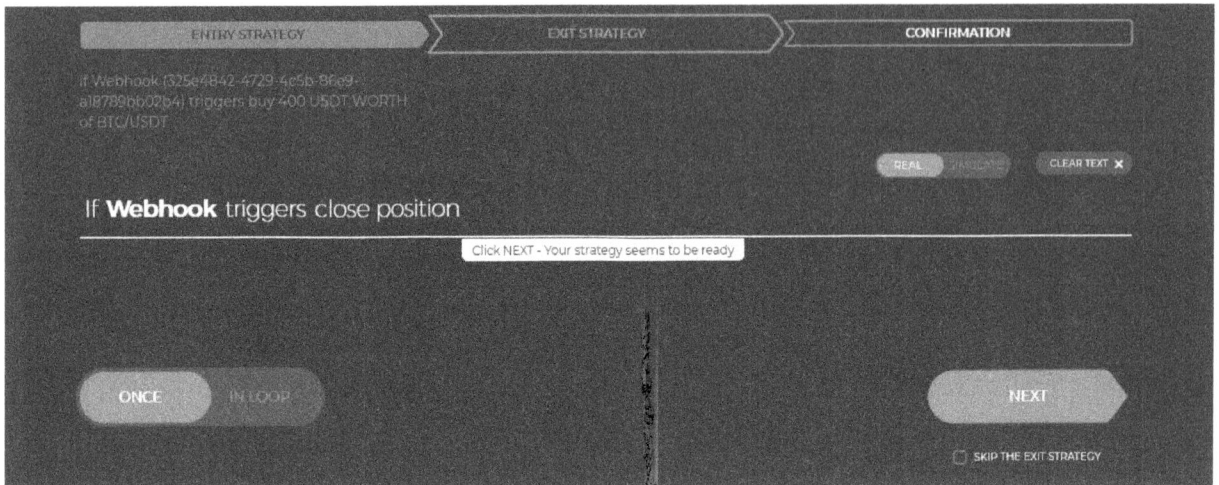

In my example I have "If webhook triggers close position". This will use your exit alert from TradingView to exit your trade. You can also add in other conditions like a stop loss.

To add a stop loss into your exit conditions you can type in the "**if at loss**" command.

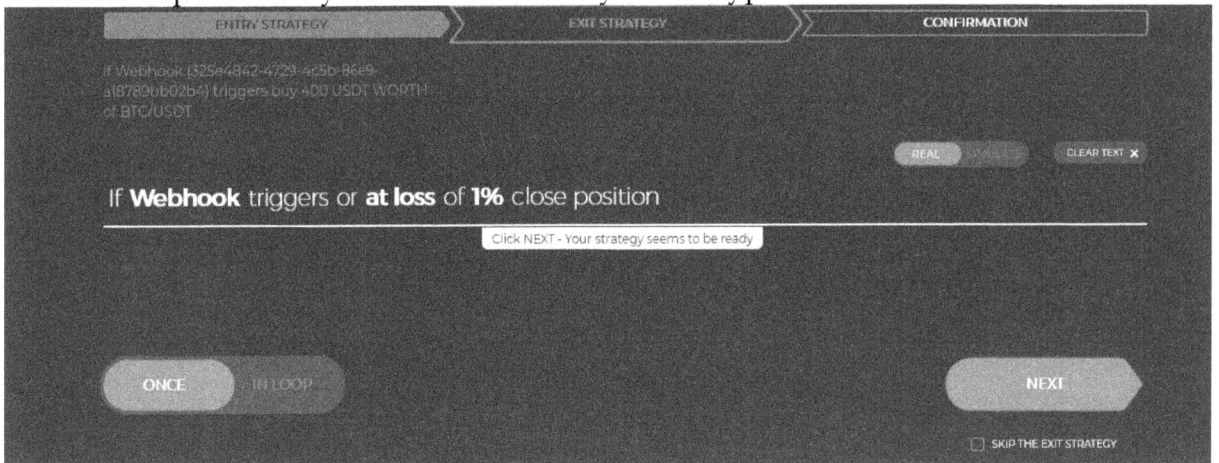

In this example I have, "If webhook triggers or at loss of 1% close position". I can use that command as my stoploss and my trade will be closed if it is at a loss of 1%.

Chapter 4: Mean Reversion Automated Trading Strategies

Mean reversion trading can be very profitable if done correctly. The markets are always moving around and identifying the extremes of those moves can provide great opportunities for traders.

A mean-reversion trading strategy uses the concept of mean reversion which is defined as a return to normal. Mean reversal analysis is based on the assumption that any given price has an intrinsic value and that it will eventually revert or "mean-revert" back to its true (intrinsic) value in the long run. The Mean Reversion Trading

How To Find The Extremes In A Price Distribution

The first step in finding a mean-reversion trading strategy is to find the extremes of a price distribution. There are several ways in which you can do this. Below, I will explain the steps in obtaining the extremes in a price distribution in relation to market prices.

1. Determine the current trend using moving averages, RSI or any other applicable tool
2. Identify extreme points in this price distribution by using overbought or oversold levels
3. Once you have identified these extremes use them as entry and exit signals for your trading strategy.

Using Overbought And Oversold Levels To Identify The Extremes Of A Price Distribution:

When trying to find a reversion trading strategy, we're essentially searching for past extremes of the price distribution. From there we can look back and identify these points of inflection (from the extreme), and then enter where the price is likely to reverse.

One way we can do this is by using a momentum oscillator that reverses as it approaches extreme readings. Can you guess what Overbought And Oversold levels on an oscillator does? It identifies the extremes of a price distribution!

Taking that into account we can try using this approach in combination with mean reversion as our starting point for building a profitable mean reversion trading strategy. On an oscillator such as the RSI you will notice that price will typically reverse once it reaches a certain level, and this is the key to building a mean reversion trading strategy.

A Example of How This Would Look:

In this example I will use a 14 period RSI (relative strength index) as my momentum oscillator. At point 1, the RSI crosses an extreme overbought level, with it going above 75. As you can see in the example below the RSI rarely goes that that high and when it does it, price typically reverses.

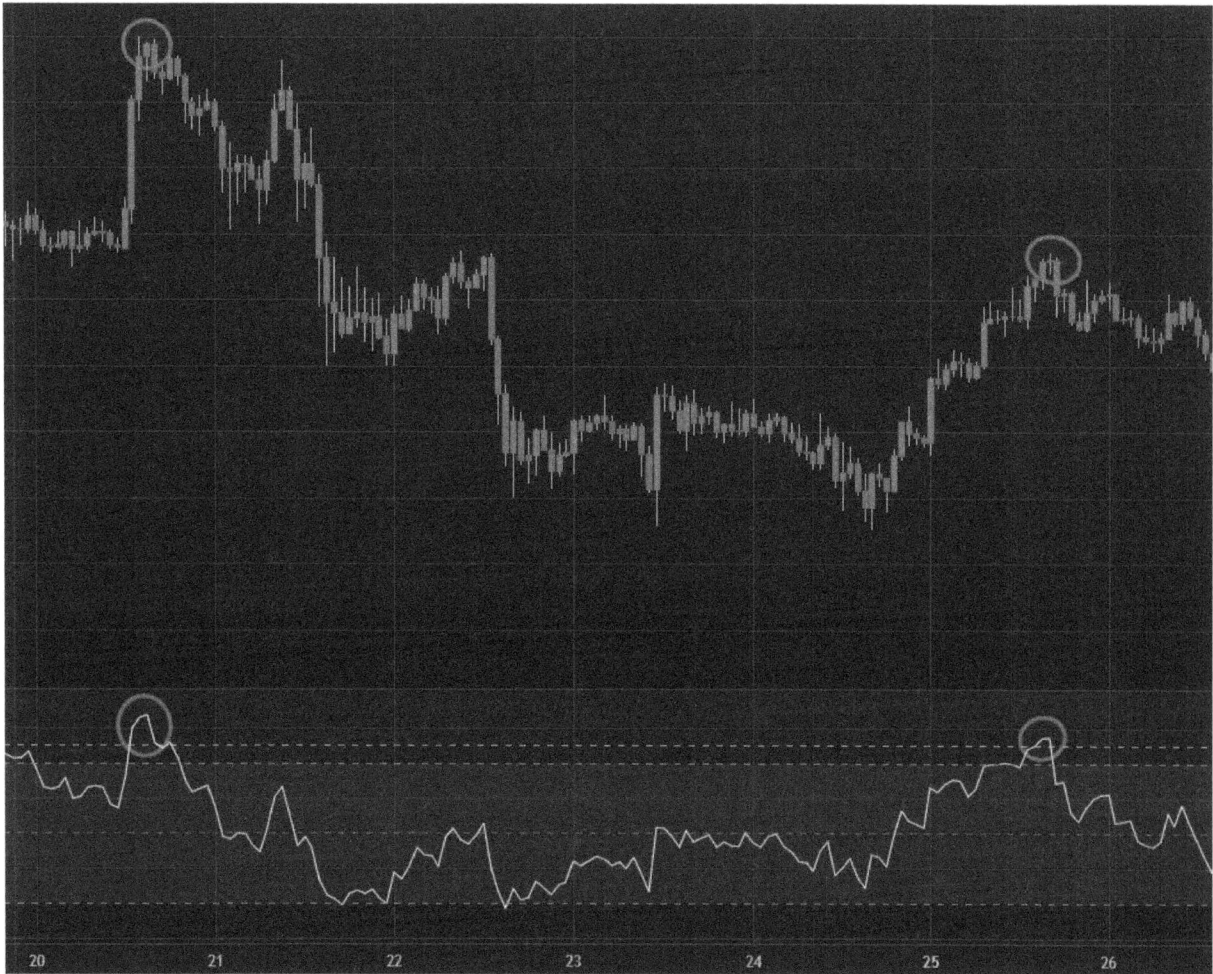

The red circles represent the RSI moving above the 75 level in this example

Only Use Mean Reversion Strategies in The Right Market Conditions

You should avoid using mean reversion strategies in strong trends since the overbought and oversold reading on oscillators will be unreliable. Mean reversion strategies are best to use when the market is moving sideways and choppy.

Mean Reversion Strategy #1: Bollinger Bands + RSI Scalping Strategy

Required Indicators:

- 4 Period RSI

- Bollinger Bands with settings:

  Length = 40, stdev = 2

Buy Conditions:

- A candle is below or touching the bottom Bollinger band

- The RSI is oversold (below 30)

- Enter trade when the RSI crosses above 30

- Place stop loss under the entry candle

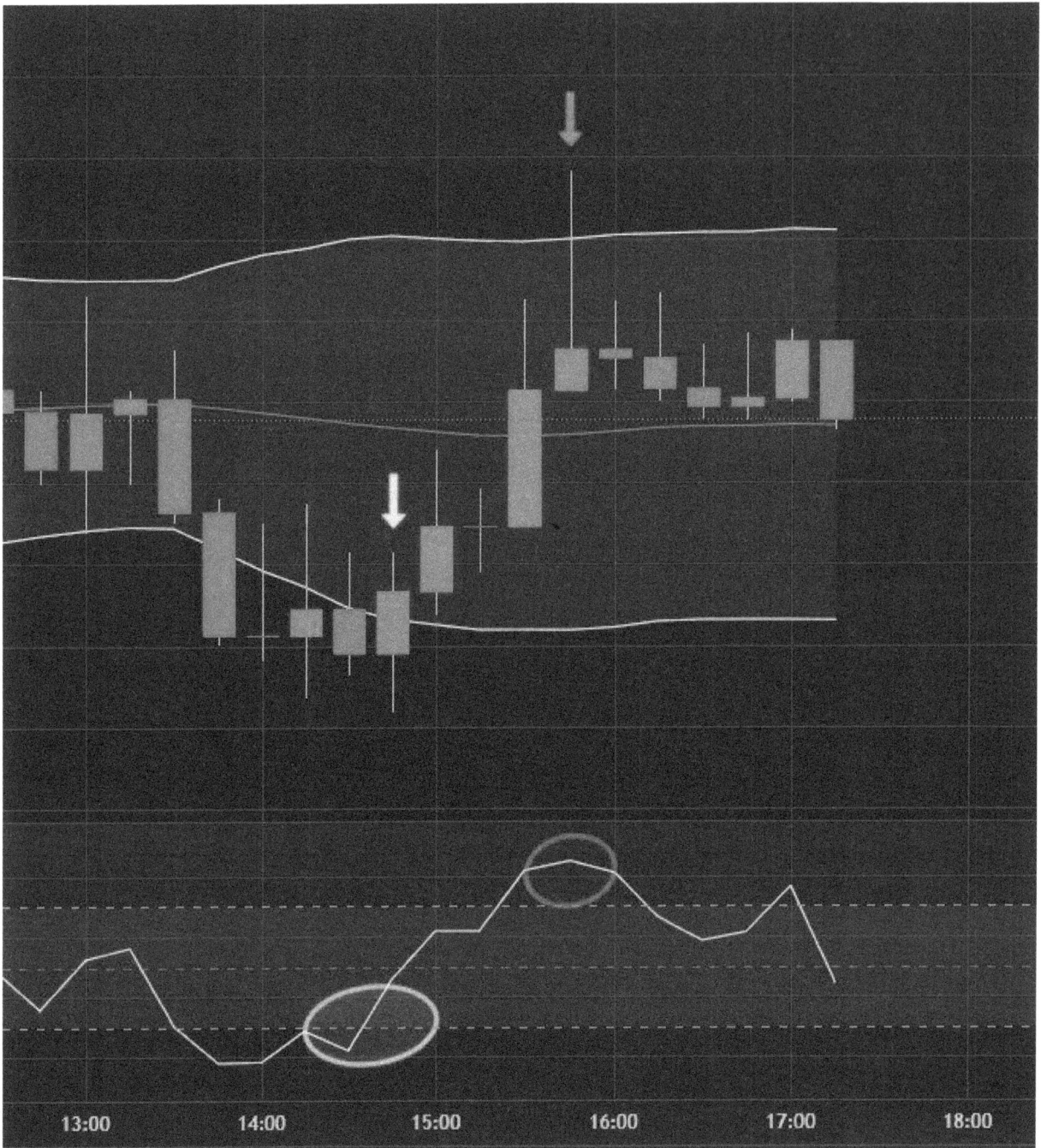

Example of a entry (green arrow) and exit (red arrow) using this strategy

Sell Conditions:

- A candle touches the top Bollinger band

OR

- The RSI crosses above 80

Mean Reversion Strategy #2: Bollinger Bands + CCI Strategy

Required Indicators:
- 20 period CCI (commodity channel index)
- Bollinger bands with settings:

   Length = 50, Stdev = 2

Buy Conditions:
- The Bollinger bands are flat and not pointing in any direction
- Price is touching or closing below the bottom band
- The CCI crosses below -200
- Buy when the CCI crosses above -200
- Place stop loss under the entry candle

Example of entry (green arrow) and exit (red arrow) using this strategy

Exit Conditions:

- Price is touching or closes above the top band

OR

- The CCI crosses below 100 after being oversold

Mean Reversion Strategy #3: Standard Deviation and RSI Scalping Strategy

Required Indicators:

- 200 SMA

- 5 period RSI

- Bollinger bands with settings:

  Stdev = 1.5, Length = 10

Long Entry Rules:

- Price is above the 200 SMA

- Candles are closing below the lower Bollinger band

- The RSI is below 30 (oversold)

- Enter long trade when the RSI crosses above 30 or a candle closes above the lower Bollinger band

- Place stop loss under the low of the entry candle

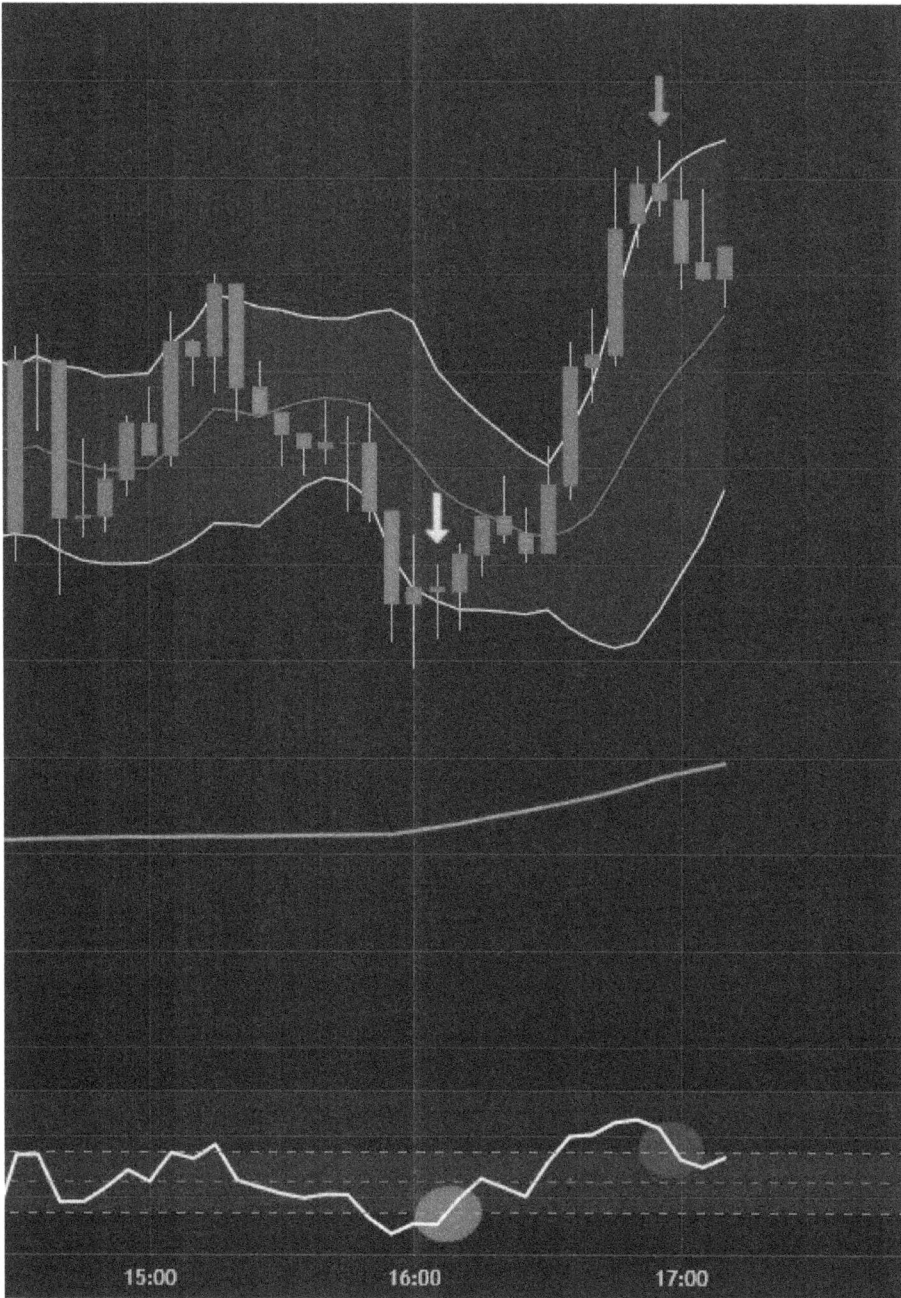

Example of a long trade using this strategy

Exit/Take Profits When:

- Price crosses above the top Bollinger band and then closes back below it

Or

- The RSI crosses above 70 (overbought), and then crosses back below 70

Short Entry Rules:

- Price is a below the 200 SMA
- Candles are closing above the top lower Bollinger band
- The RSI is above 70 (overbought)
- Enter short trade when the RSI crosses below 70 or a candle closes below the top Bollinger band
- Place stop loss under the low of the entry candle

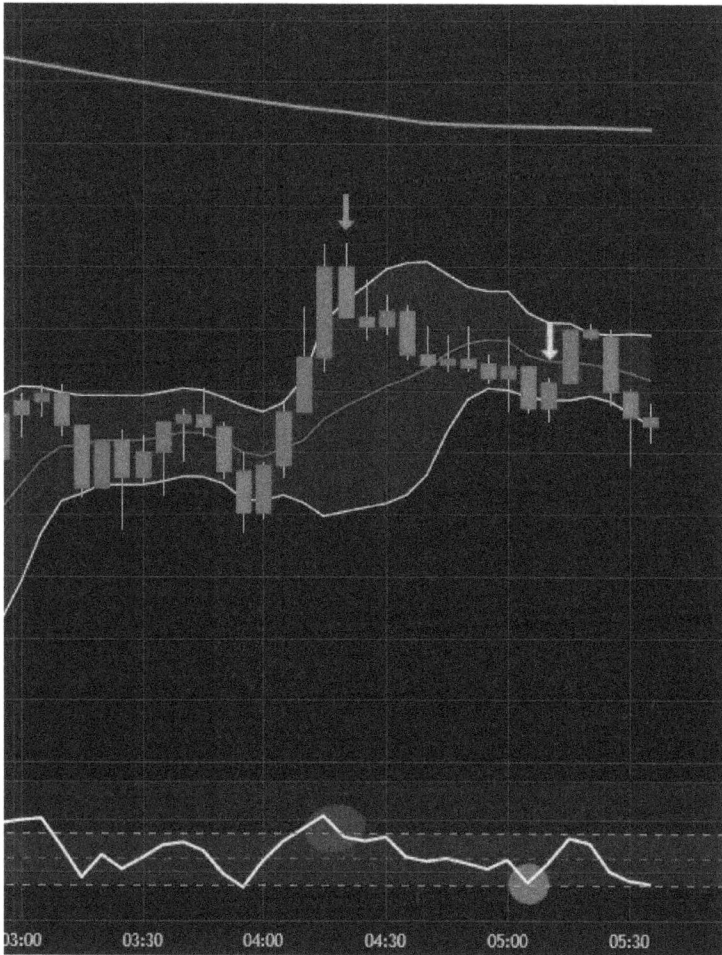

Example of a short trade using this strategy

Exit/Take Profits When:

- Price crosses below bottom Bollinger band and then closes back above it

Or

- The RSI is crosses below 30 (oversold) and then crosses back above 30

Mean Reversion Strategy #4: RSI Mean Reversion Strategy

Required Indicators

- 25 HMA (Hull moving average)

- RSI, Length = 14

- Bollinger bands added on the RSI

  Bollinger bands settings: Length = 40, StDev = 1

The RSI should look like the example below

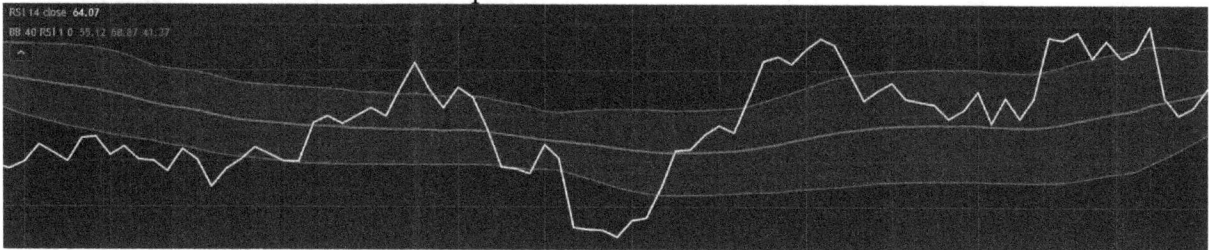

Buy Conditions

- The RSI crosses above the lower Bollinger band
- Candles are closing above the 25 HMA

Example of a buy signal (green circle) and sell signal (red circle) using this strategy

Exit Conditions:

- A candle closes below the 25 HMA

Or

- The RSI crosses below the upper band from above

Mean Reversion Strategy #5: Stochastic Mean Reversion Strategy

Required Indicators:

- 30 HMA (Hull moving average)

- Stochastic with settings:

  %K = 14, %K smooth = 6, %D = 3

Buy Conditions:

- The Stochastics are below 30 and crossed up

- Buy when a candle closes above the HMA

- Place stop loss under the entry candle

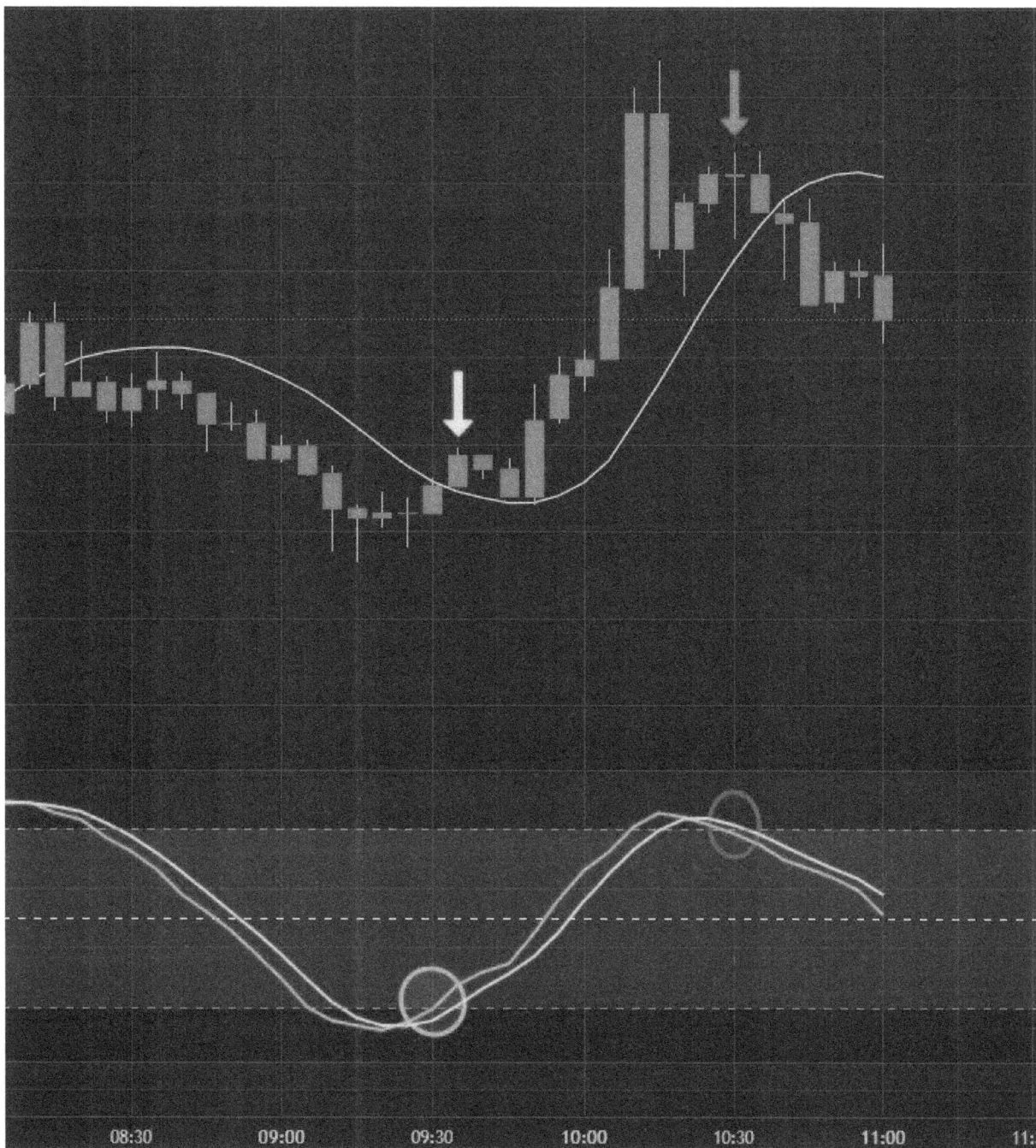

Example of a entry (green arrow) and exit (red arrow) using this strategy

Sell Conditions:

- The stochastic is crossing down from above 70

OR

- A candle closes below the HMA

Chapter 5: Moving Average Based Trading Strategies

Moving averages are the most common indicators used in automated trading. They are intuitive to implement and can be extremely effective when used correctly. The biggest advantage of employing moving averages in an automated trading strategy is that you can capitalize quickly on emerging trends.

When prices move above their moving averages it indicates an upward trend, while when they fall below their moving averages it indicates a downward trend. A moving average can smooth out the random fluctuations in stock prices and highlight any trends, momentum and support/resistance that may be present in the market.

Combine this with strict stop loss and profit-taking rules and you could have a very profitable trading strategy.

Trading Strategy Using Cross-over Signal

A cross-over signal occurs when two indicators cross each other, either above or below each other. This is another way to generate a trading signal for your strategy. A cross-over cross can be used to determine the general direction of price movement, but it should not be the only indicator that you look at when making trading decisions.

Using Cross-Over Signals for entry and exit signals:

The simplest way to use cross-over signals would be buy when the fast moving average crosses above the slow moving average, and sell when the fast crosses below the slow moving average.

Alternatively, you could set your stop loss order under the slow period moving average and your take profit order above the fast period moving average.

Creating a Robust Trading Strategy Using MA Crossovers

You can combine a cross-over signal with a trend line break to create a more robust trading strategy; simply look for the two conditions below:

1) The price breaks through an identified resistance level

AND

2) The slow MA is positioned under the fast MA and starts to move up (a cross-over signal). This identifies that there is clear bullish momentum happening as indicated by both the trend breaking and the movement of the fast MAs crossovers.

When selling, look for these criteria:

1) The price breaks through an identified support level

AND

2) The slow MA is positioned above the fast MA and starts to move down (another cross-over signal).

This identifies that there is clear bearish momentum happening as indicated by both the trend breaking and the movement of the fast MAs crossovers.

An example of how this would look:

We want to buy when the 7 period SMA crosses above the 15 period SMA AND the 34 period SMA is above the 80 period SMA
We will set our stop loss at 2% below the entry candle and exit the trade when the 7 SMA crosses below the 10 SMA OR a candle closes under the 15 SMA.

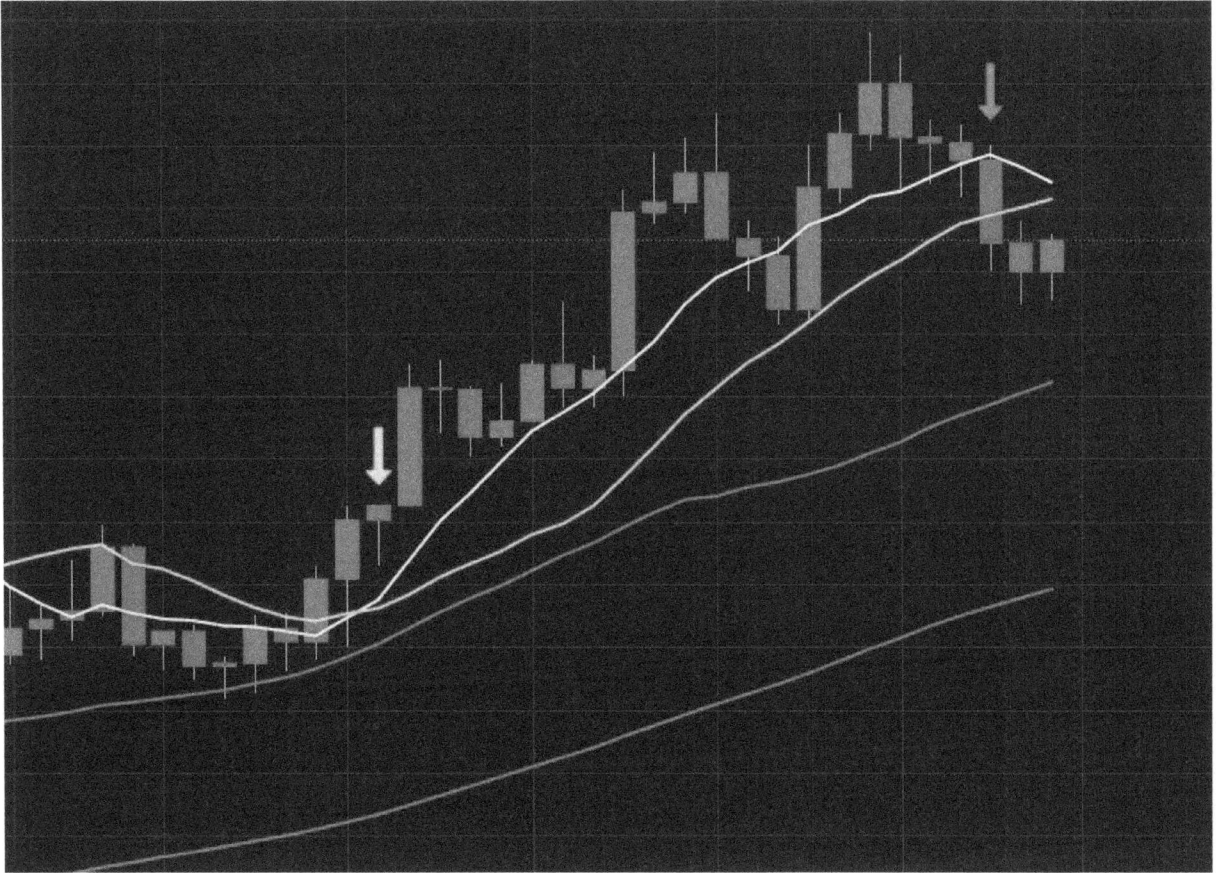

Here, we determine that we will enter a long trade when our 4 moving averages indicate upward momentum, and exit once the market begins trending downward or once we reach our profit target.

This is based on simple price action: if both short and long-term moving averages are pointing in the same direction, it indicates strong momentum which may lead to an increase in price. Exiting when this momentum begins to diminish helps to ensure a profitable trade.

Using Price Crossovers

Another good moving average strategy for using in your system is to use price crossovers of moving averages, this can be used to generate more accurate buy and sell signals then MA crossovers.

This technique involves using one moving average specifically for entering the trade, a entry signal will be when price closes a bar above the specified MA (usually a longer period MA), and for exiting you will use another MA (usually a shorter period).

For example:

We will use a 10 SMA and a 20 SMA, and the 10 SMA must be above the 20 SMA. Our buy signal will be when a candle crosses and closes above the 20 period SMA. We will use a candle crossing and closing below the 10 SMA as a sell signal.

This is a very simple concept, but it can generate a lot of profit if used properly.

The most commonly used types of moving averages include:

The Simple moving average (SMA), exponential moving average (EMA) and weighted moving average (WMA).

Simple Moving Average (SMA) – A SMA is calculated by adding up the prices of a security over some time period and then dividing this total by the number of prices used in the calculation. The result you get will be the average price of the security during that specific time period

Exponential Moving Average (EMA) –An EMA has a weight assigned to each data point, which determines how much influence that particular price will have on the moving average for a given time period.

For example, a weighting factor of 0.5 means that each piece of new information decreases the impact of all previous pieces to 50 percent. As more new data comes in, the impact of older data diminishes.

Weighted Moving Average (WMA) –A WMA assigns each price a weighting factor based on how old that price is, so the closer a given periods closing price is to the current time, the greater its weighting factor.

A WMA calculation will mean that more recent prices are given proportionately more importance than prices from the past. That's why moving averages are so useful, they help to smooth out price fluctuations and give you a clearer picture of what the market is currently doing.

Choosing a Moving Average

After deciding the type of moving average you want to use, you should consider how long your moving average should be. There is no general rule here and many different factors will play a role in determining the length of time for your moving average (for example: short-term vs long-term trends, trading style etc.). In general, short-term moving averages are more sensitive to price changes and therefore more reactive. Conversely, long-term moving averages are less sensitive to price changes but react more gradually. Moving averages can provide a good entry or exit point for the market since they help you identify uptrends and downtrends by looking at the direction of their movement (they easily show where the trend is heading).

Moving Average Strategy #1: Easy SMA Scalping Strategy

Required Indicators:

- 9 SMA (simple moving average)
- 18 SMA

Buy Conditions:

- The 9 SMA is above the 18 SMA
- Enter when a candle crosses above and closes above the 18 SMA
- Place stop loss under the low of the entry candle

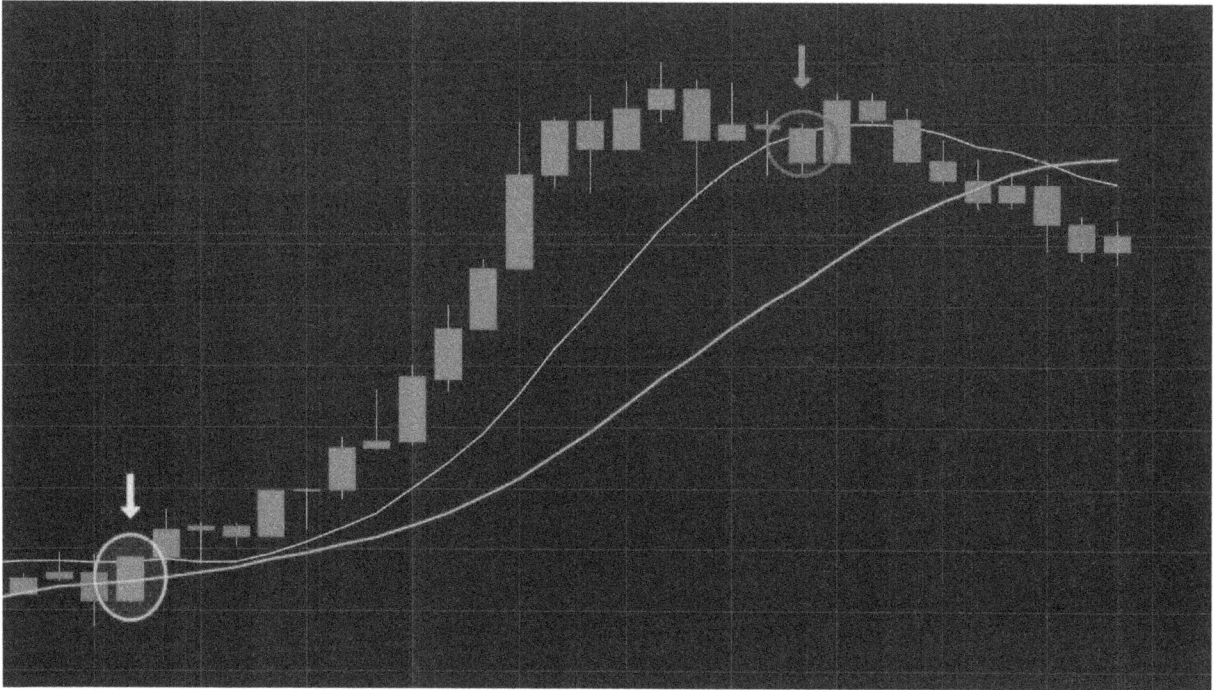

An example of a buy entry (green arrow) and exit (red arrow) using this strategy

Sell Conditions:

- A candle closes below the 9 SMA

Moving Average Strategy #2: Hull Moving Average Strategy

Required Indicators:
- 30 period Hull moving average (HMA)

- Stochastic with settings:

  %K Length = 14, %K Smoothing = 6, %D Smoothing= 3

Buy Conditions:

- The stochastics are crossed up and below 50

- Enter when a candle closes above the HMA

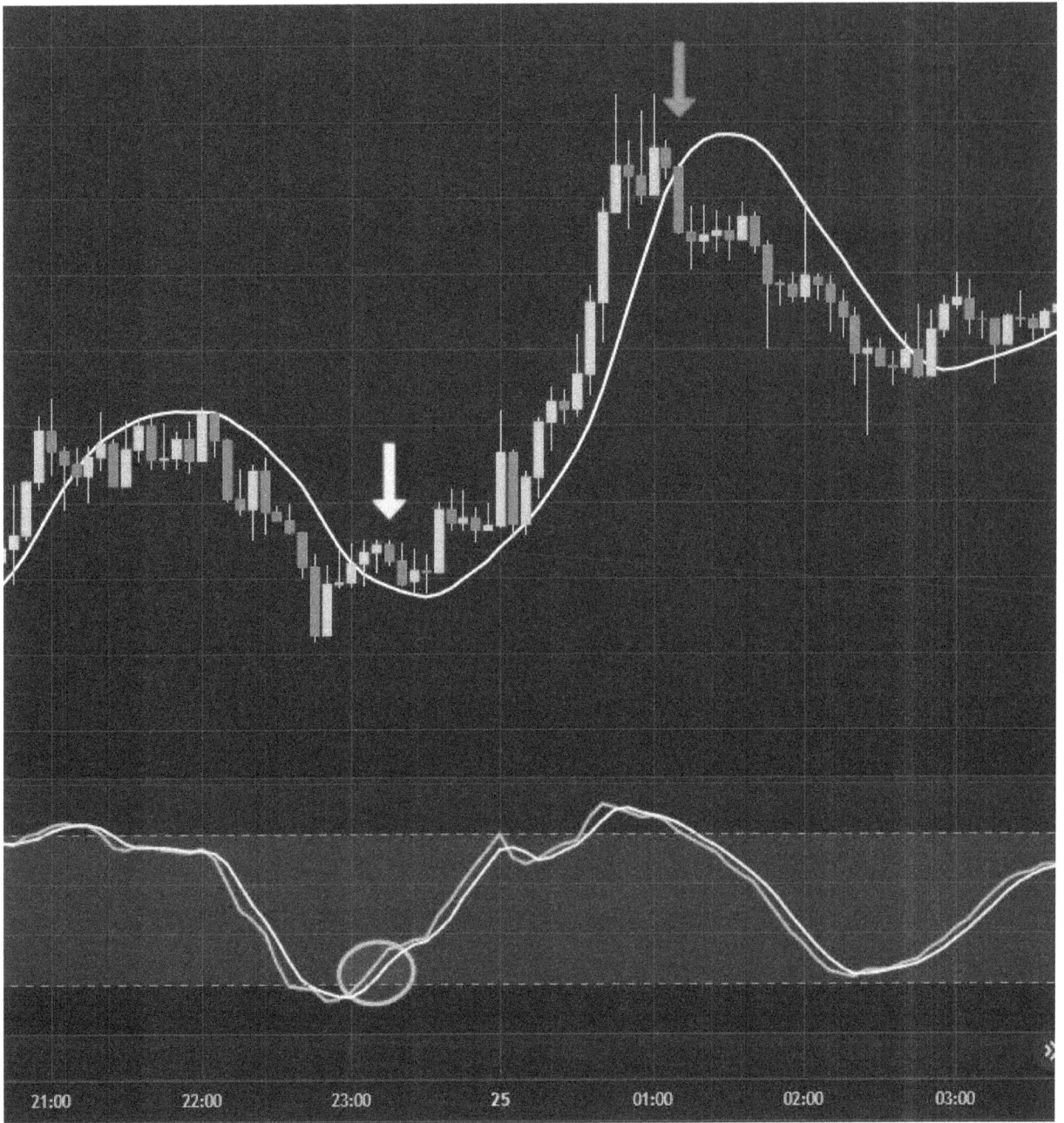

Example of a entry (green arrow) and exit signal (red arrow) using this strategy

Exit Conditions:

- A candle closes below the HMA

Moving Average Strategy #3: 4x SMA Crossover Trading System

Required Indicators

- 10 SMA
- 25 SMA
- 5 SMA
- 10 SMA

Buy Conditions:

- The 10 SMA crosses above the 25 SMA
- Buy when price touches the 25 SMA after the crossover
- Place stop loss under the entry candle

Example of a buy entry using this strategy

Sell Conditions:

- The 5 SMA crosses below the 10 SMA

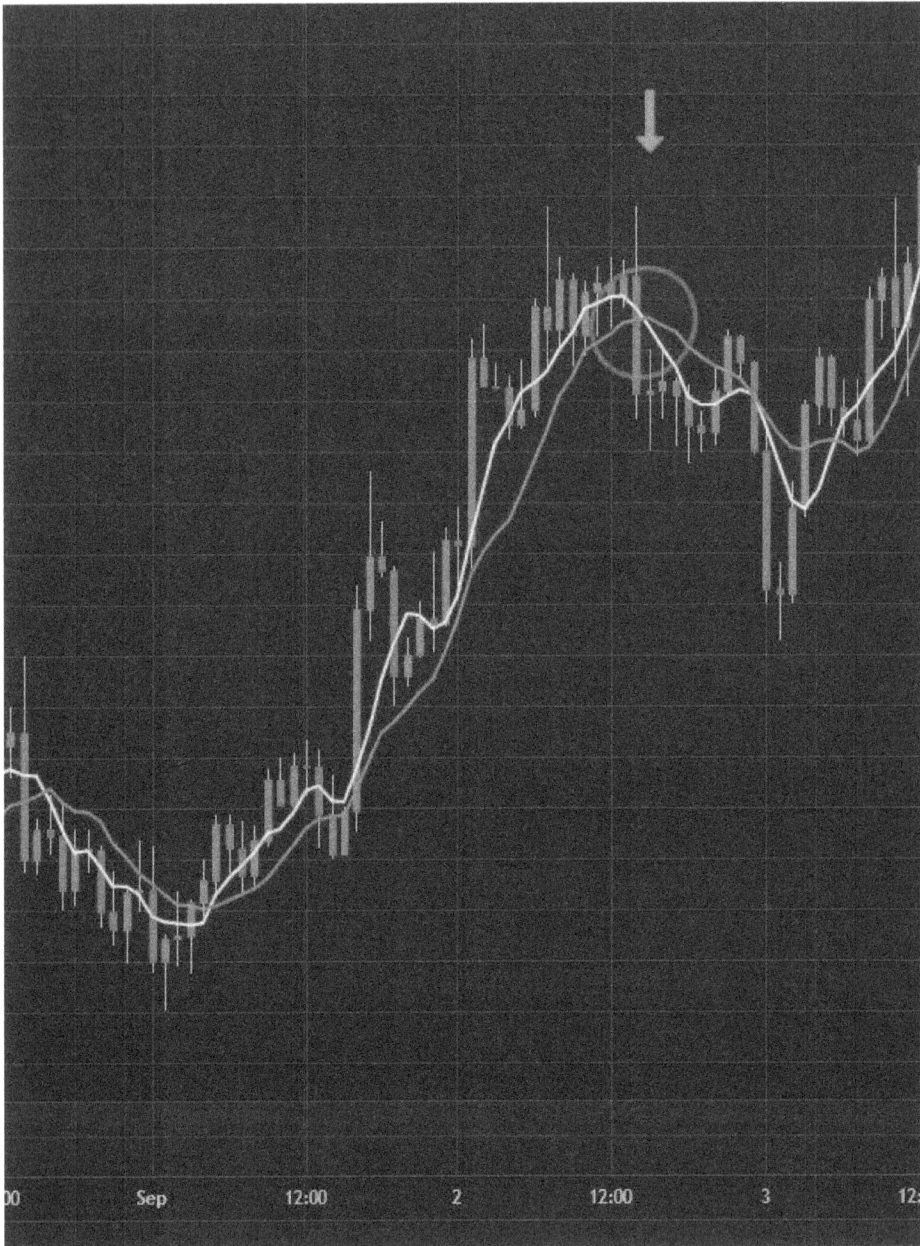

Example of a exit signal using this strategy

Moving Average Strategy #4: 45 SMA + 15 SMA Crossover Strategy

Required Indicators:

- 15 SMA
- 45 SMA
- 5 period RSI

Buy Conditions:

- The 15 SMA crosses above the 45 SMA
- Enter when the RSI crosses above 30
- Place stop loss under the last swing low

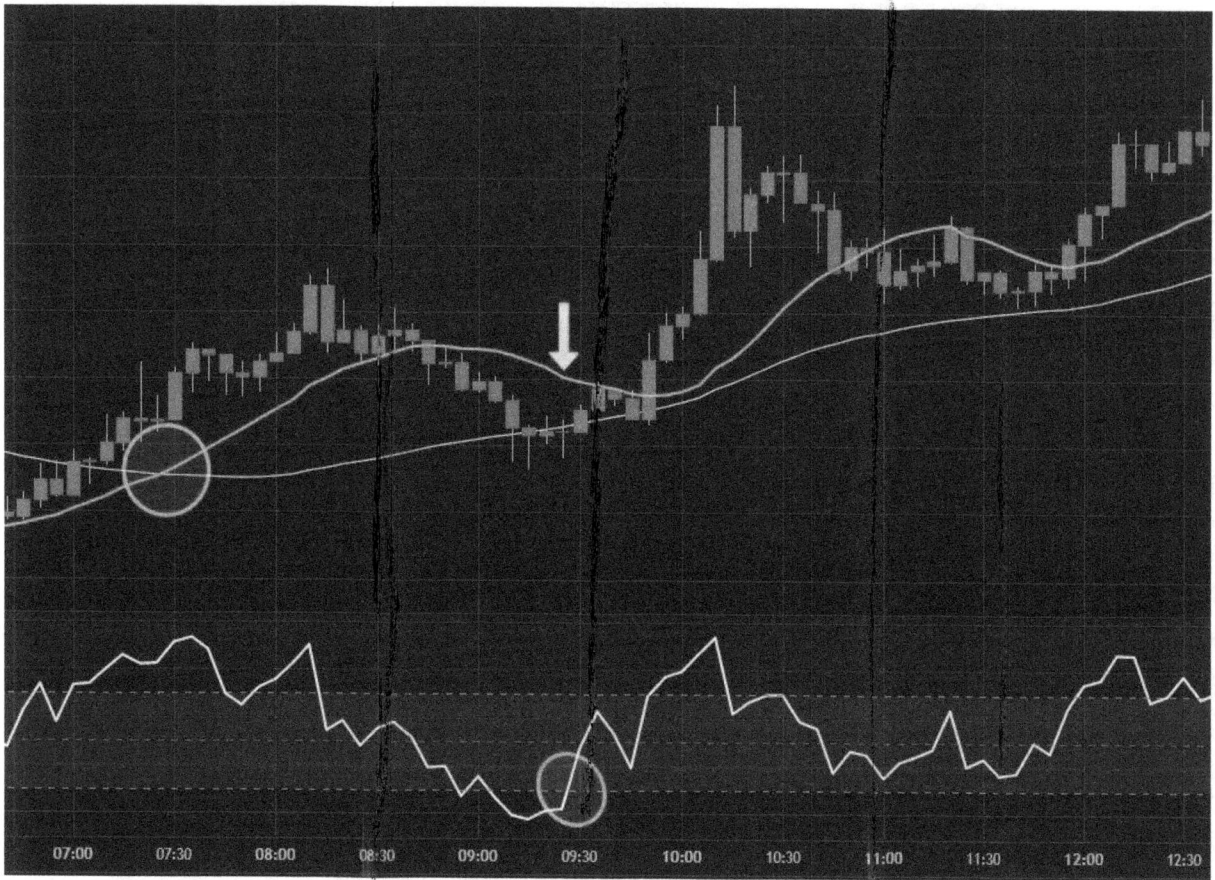

Example of a buy signal using this strategy

Sell Conditions:

- The RSI crosses below 70 after being overbought (recommended for scalping)

OR

- The 15 SMA crosses below the 45 SMA (recommended for swing trading)

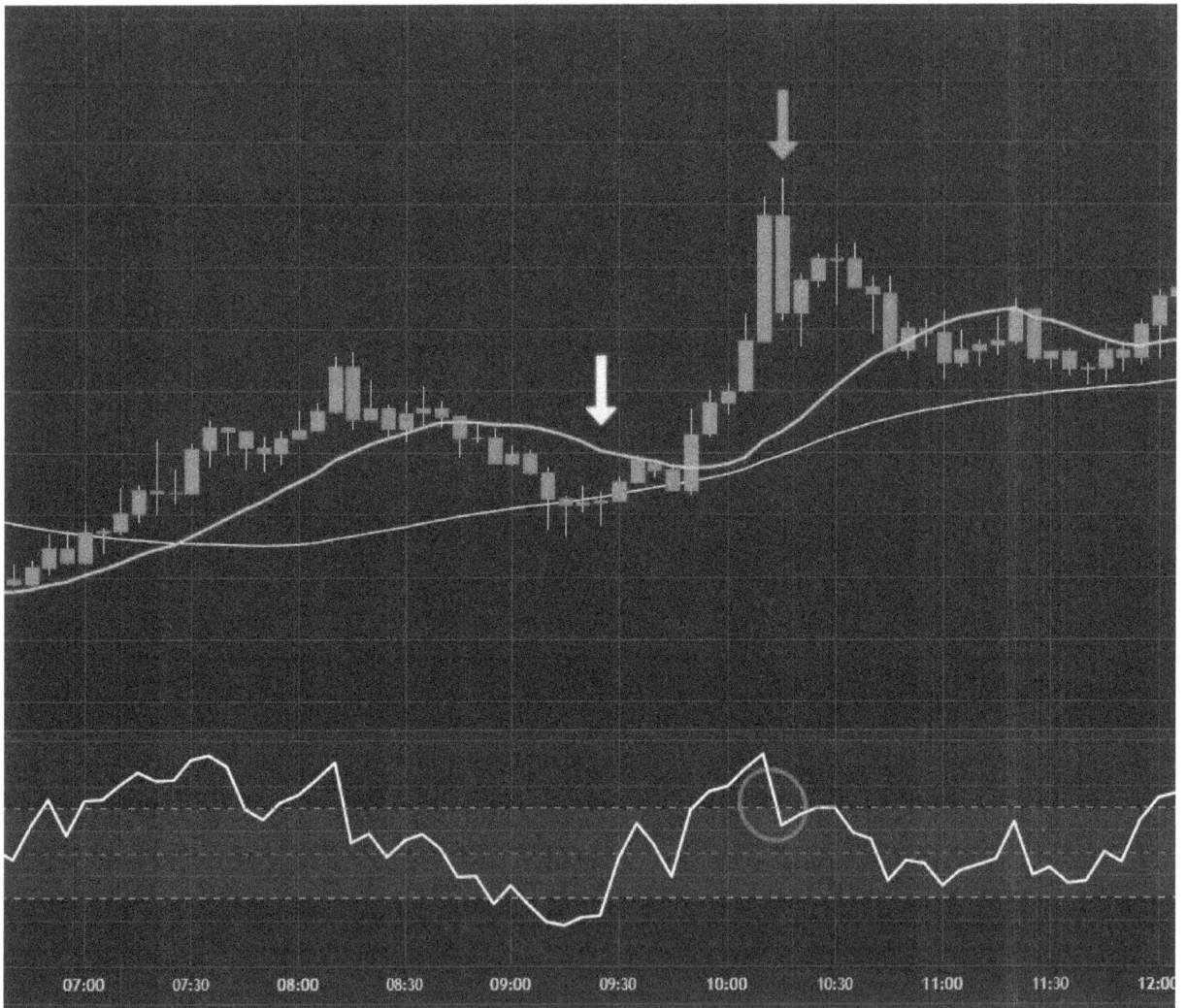

Example of a exit signal (red arrow) using this strategy

Moving Average Strategy #5: SMMA + RSI Strategy

Required Indicators

- 6 SMMA (smoothed moving average)

- 14 period RSI

  Add a 40 period DEMA (double exponential moving average) on the RSI

Buy Conditions:

- The RSI crosses above the DEMA

- Enter trade when a candle closes above the SMMA, place a stop loss under the entry candle

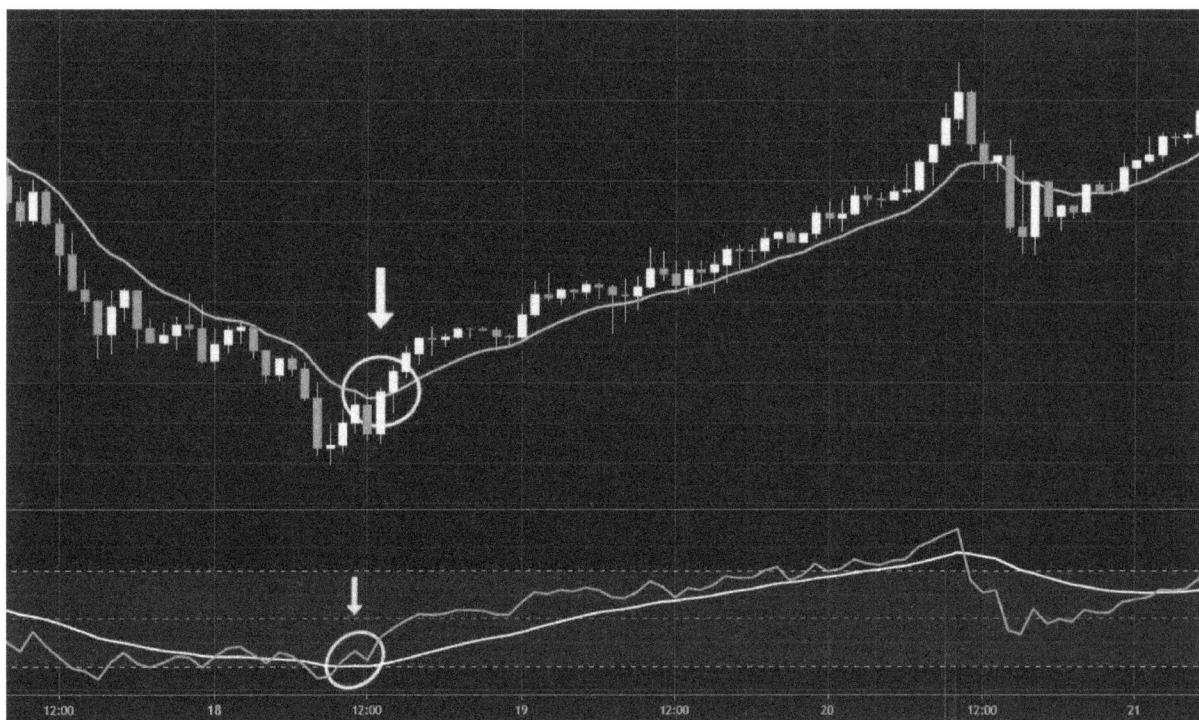

Example of a buy signal using this strategy

Exit Conditions:

- A candle closes below the SMMA

Or

- The RSI crosses below the DEMA

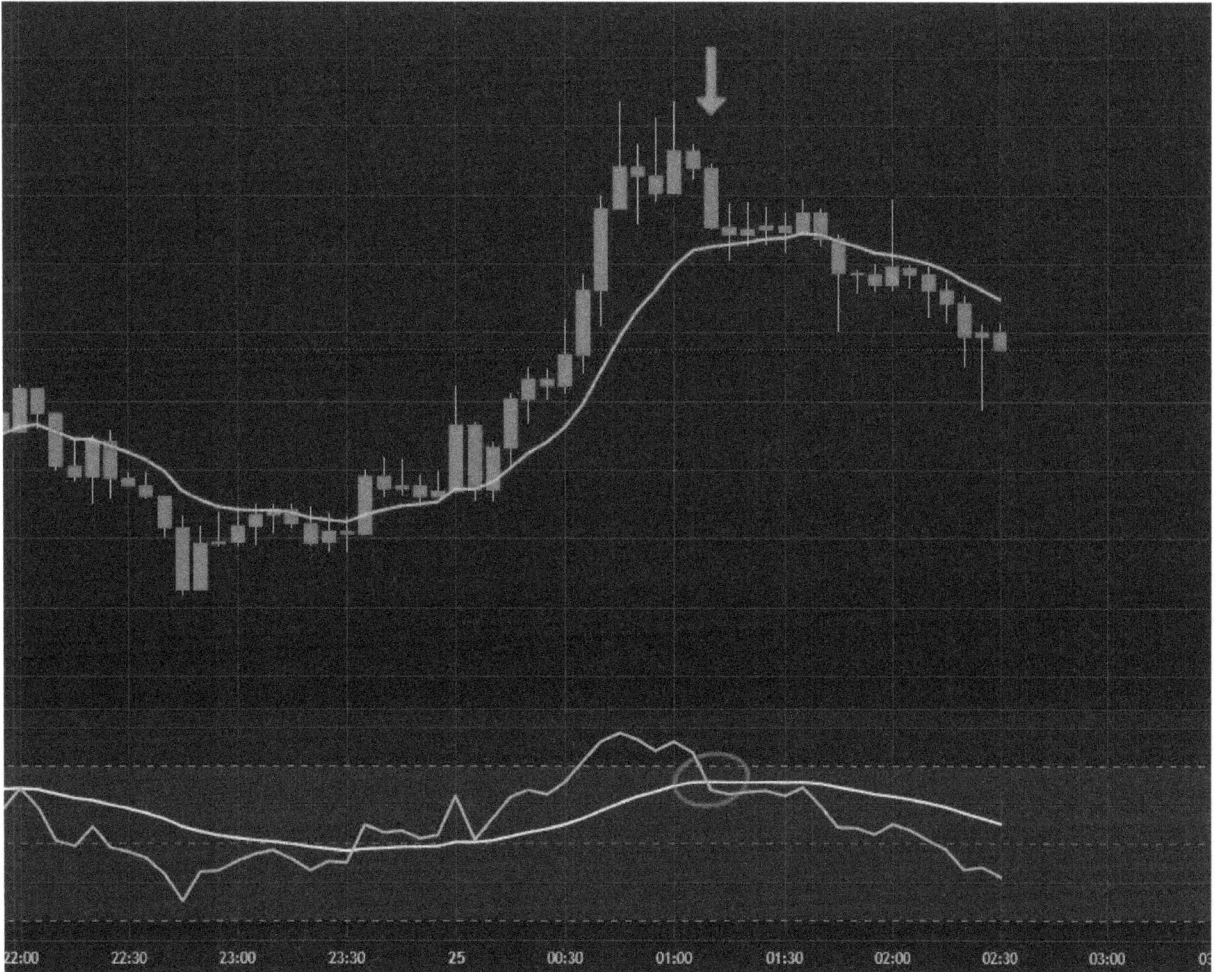

Example of a sell signal using this strategy

Moving Average Strategy #6: WMA Crossover System

Required Indicators

- 40 WMA (weighted moving average)
- 60 WMA
- 210 WMA

Buy Conditions:

- Price is above all moving averages
- The 210 WMA is slopped upward
- The 40 WMA is above the 60 WMA
- Enter long trade when 60 WMA crosses above the 210 WMA
- Set stop loss below the last swing low

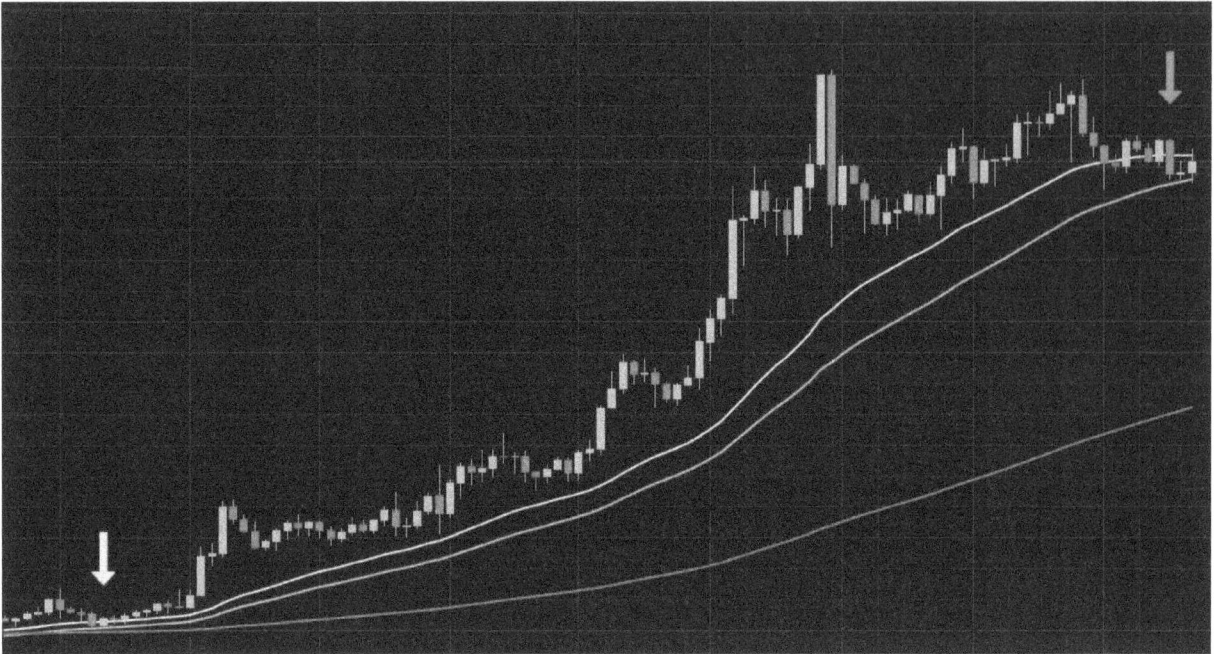

Example of a long trade using this strategy

Exit Conditions:

- Exit trade when price closes below the 40 WMA

Moving Average Strategy #7: Smoothed Moving Average Crossover Strategy

Required Indicators:
- 9 SMMA (smoothed moving average)
- 4 SMMA
- 15 SMA

Buy Conditions

- The 4 SMMA crosses above the 9 SMMA
- Enter when a candle touches the 4 SMMA and closes above it
- Place stop loss under the low of the entry candle

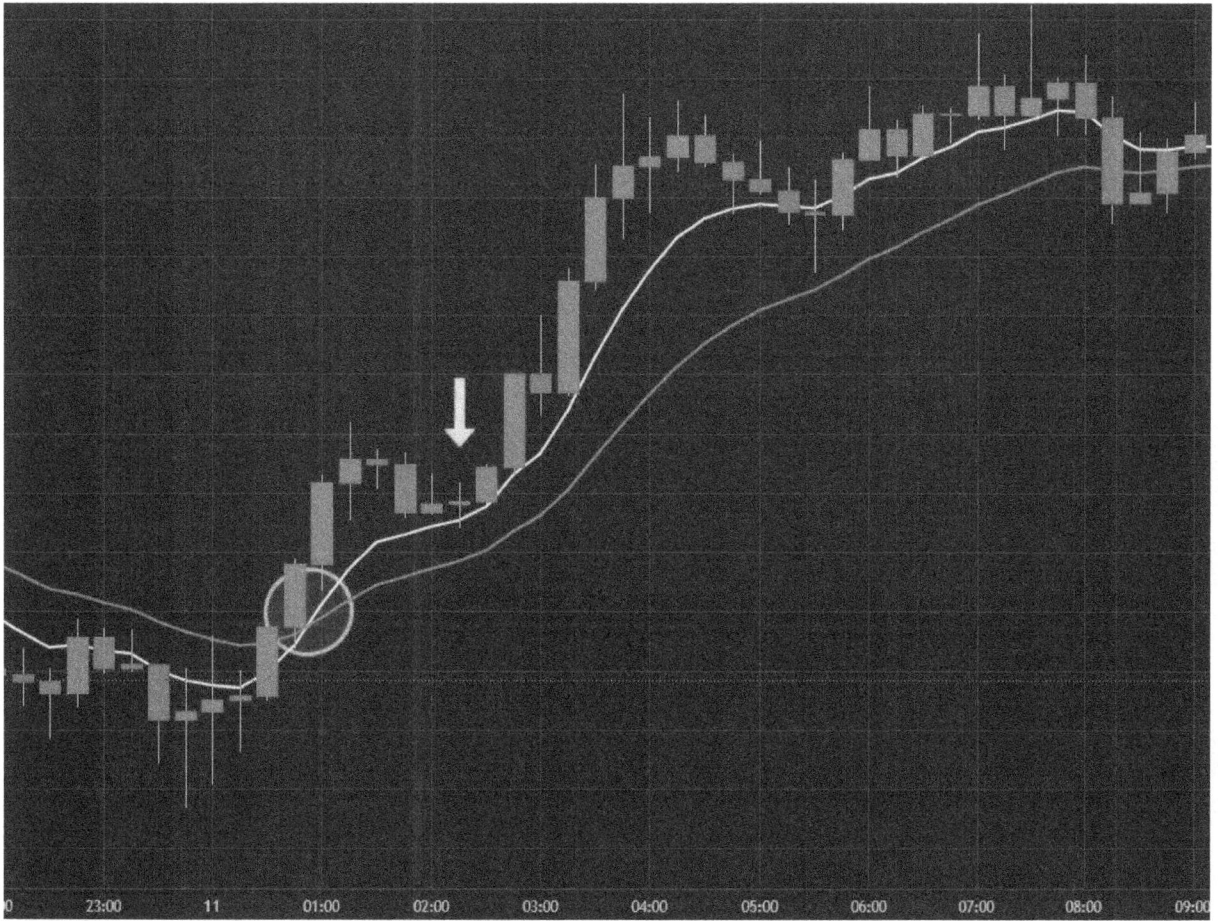

Example of a buy signal using this strategy

Exit Conditions:

- A candle closes below the 15 SMA

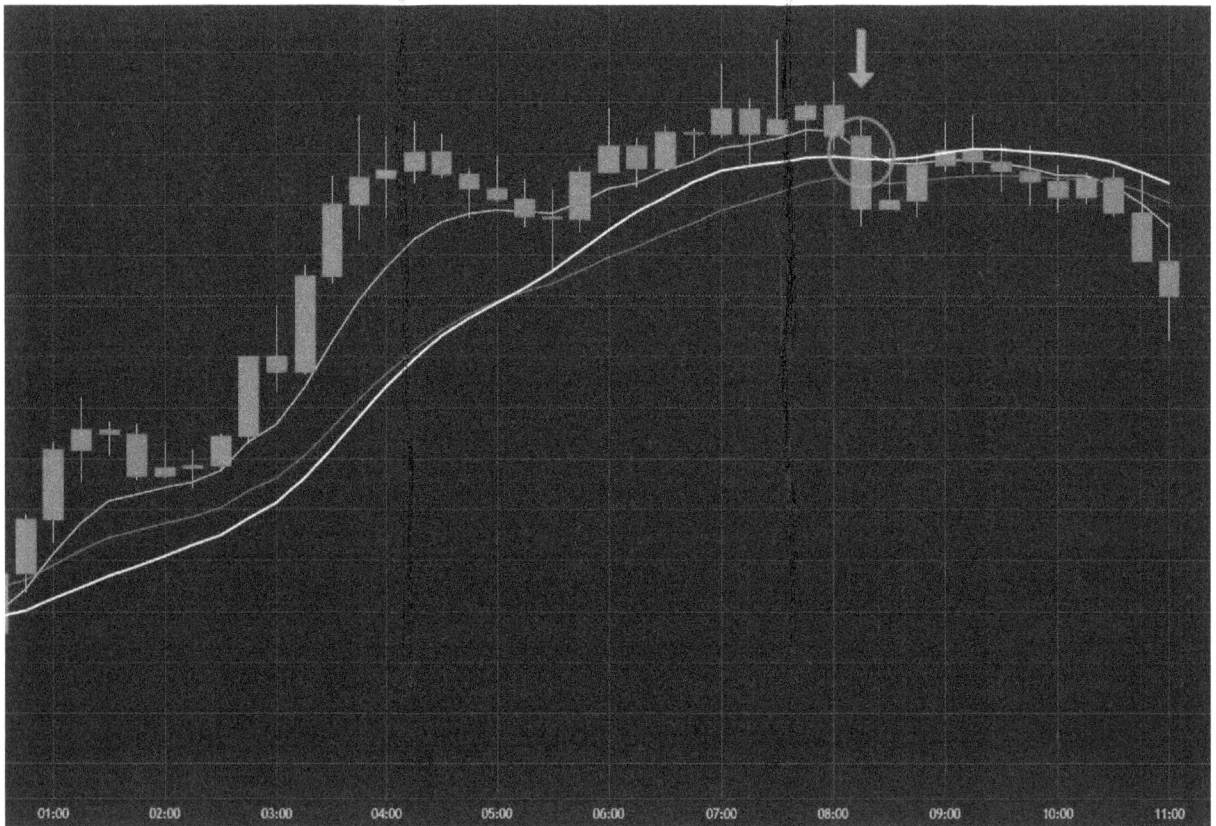

Example of a sell signal using this strategy

Moving Average Strategy #8: Bollinger Band + HMA Strategy

Required Indicators:

- 15 period HMA (Hull moving average)
- 5 period RSI
- Bollinger bands with settings

  Length = 20, Stdev = 2.5

Buy/Long Conditions:

- The RSI is oversold
- A candle is below or touching the bottom Bollinger band
- Buy when a candle closes above the HMA

Example of an entry (green arrow) and exit (red arrow) for a long trade using this strategy

Exit Long Rules:

- The RSI is overbought

Or

- A candle closes below the HMA

Sell/Short Conditions:

- The RSI is overbought
- A candle is above or touching the top Bollinger band
- Short when a candle closes below the HMA

Exit Short When:

- The RSI is oversold

Or

- A candle closes above the HMA

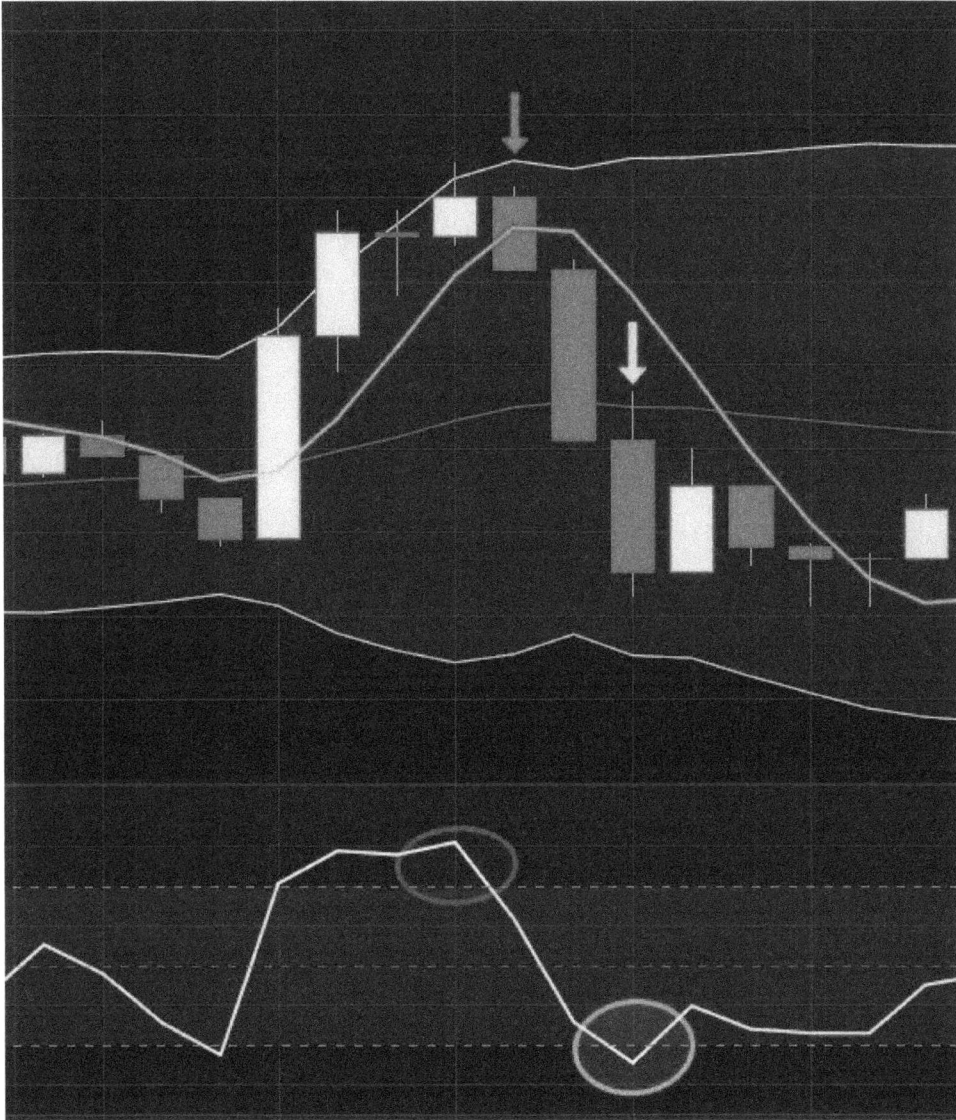

Example of an entry (red arrow) and exit (green arrow) for a short trade using this strategy

Moving Average Strategy #9: 1 Minute Moving Average Scalping Strategy

This strategy is designed for using on the 1 minute timeframe

Required Indicators:

- 200 EMA

- 1000 sma (simple moving average)

- Stochastic with settings:

  K = 14, D = 3, Smooth K = 6

Buy Conditions:

- The 200 EMA is above the 1000 SMA

- Price drops below the 200 EMA

- The stochastics are below 20

- Buy when a candle touches the 1000 SMA, place a stop loss under the low of the entry candle

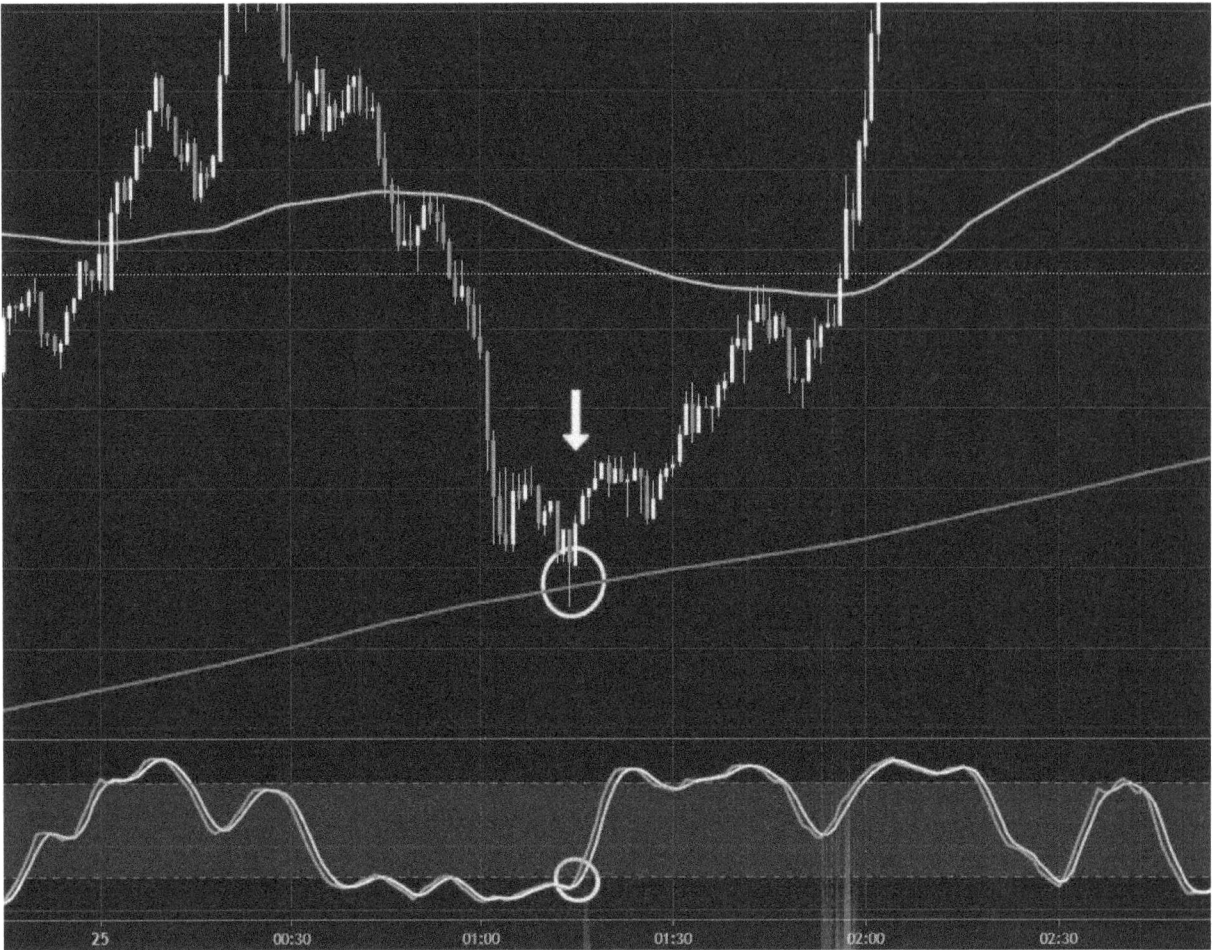

Example of a buy signal using this strategy

Exit Conditions:

- Price touches the 200 EMA

www.ingramcontent.com/pod-product-compliance
Lightning Source LLC
Chambersburg PA
CBHW082009190326
41458CB00010B/3135